UNITED NO MORE!

STORIES OF THE CIVIL WAR

by Doreen Rappaport and Joan Verniero

illustrated by Rick Reeves

HarperCollins*Publishers*

Library of Congress Cataloging-in-Publication Data
Rappaport, Doreen.
United no more! : stories of the Civil War / by Doreen Rappaport
and Joan Verniero ; illustrated by Rick Reeves.— 1st ed.
    p. cm.
Includes index.
ISBN-10: 0-06-050599-0—ISBN-10: 0-06-050600-8 (lib. bdg.)
ISBN-13: 978-0-06-050599-8—ISBN-13: 978-0-06-050600-1
(lib. bdg.)
    1. United States—History—Civil War, 1861–1865—
Anecdotes—Juvenile literature. 2. United States—History—
Civil War, 1861–1865—Biography—Juvenile literature. I.
Verniero, Joan C. II. Reeves, Rick, ill. III. Title.
E655R27 2006
973.7—dc22
                                                    2005005724

Typography by Larissa Lawrynenko
1 2 3 4 5 6 7 8 9 10

First Edition

For my dear friend Sharon Harrison,
and my expert reader, Kevin Cote
—D.R.

For Dorothy Carter, friend, author,
educator, inspiration
—J.V.

CONTENTS

ABOUT THIS BOOK

Immediately after Abraham Lincoln's election as president in November 1860, long-standing differences and tensions between the South and North erupted. Before Christmas seven Southern states seceded, or withdrew, from the Union, beginning with South Carolina. Jefferson Davis was elected president of the new Confederate States of America.

Davis declared that Fort Sumter now belonged to the Confederacy. The federal fort stood on an island in the center of the important Charleston harbor. Major Robert Anderson and his sixty-eight Union soldiers refused to evacuate Fort Sumter. On April 12, 1861, Confederate troops fired on the fort. After thirty-four hours of bombardment, Anderson surrendered. The Union Stars and Stripes was taken down and replaced by the Confederate Stars and Bars. During late April and May, four more Southern states seceded from the Union.

The United States was *united no more*. For the next four years, men and women in the North and in the South fought for what they believed. Brothers fought against brothers; fathers fought against sons. Both sides amassed armies. Both sides had their own flag. Both had their own lyrics, but their songs shared popular melodies. This book contains stories about Americans on both sides.

Julia Ward Howe was a poet from Massachusetts and a staunch believer in the Union. On November 18, 1861, she went to the

Virginia hills to see a military review of the Grand Army of the Potomac. The discipline and determination of the soldiers inspired her. At dawn the next morning, in the dim light of her hotel room, she wrote a poem with only the nib of a pen. "The Battle Hymn of the Republic" was written to the tune of a Southern hymn. It became the North's battle cry.

Women in the South were equally committed to their cause. On April 25, 1862, the victorious Union forces raised the Stars and Stripes in New Orleans, Louisiana. Union soldiers poured into the city. Southern women made life as difficult as they could for these soldiers. Eugenia Phillips, a Southerner, hated the Northern occupiers. Mrs. Phillips was arrested and jailed in primitive, humiliating conditions. It did not break her spirit.

The war dragged on. Southerners suffered from shortages of food and paid high prices for what little was available. On April 2, 1863, the women of Richmond, Virginia, took to the streets to protest unfair prices, chanting "Bread or blood!"

Black Americans—free and enslaved—fought for the Union. Slaves ran away to join the army. At first they were not allowed to fight. They had to dig ditches, build fortifications, and serve the officers. Free blacks tried to enlist at the war's beginning. President Lincoln resisted. He feared that the border states in the Union would secede if black men were allowed to pick up arms. Northern abolitionists—people who were against slavery—pressed for them to be taken into the army.

The first black regiments were mustered in Louisiana. Then Rhode Island, Kansas, and Massachusetts called for black troops. On October 28, 1862, the 79th U.S. Colored Infantry (1st Kansas) became the first unit of black men to go into battle. On July 18, 1863, the Massachusetts 54th Colored Infantry led a heroic charge at Fort Wagner, South Carolina. Though wounded three times, Sergeant William H. Carney of New Bedford, Massachusetts, saved the American flag from capture. He was the first person of African descent to be awarded the Congressional Medal of Honor.

Many Southern-born officers had served in the Union armed forces before the Civil War and chose to fight with the Confederacy once the war began. Robert E. Lee's leadership and dignity inspired Southern troops, even when defeat seemed inevitable. Other Southerners, such as David Glasgow Farragut, remained loyal to the Union. His victories at New Orleans and Mobile Bay, Alabama, gave hope to Northerners.

By March 1865 Union victories in Savannah, Georgia; Columbia and Charleston, South Carolina; and Wilmington, North Carolina, made Northerners feel victory was close. But they worried if the country could be unified after such a brutal, divisive war. In his Second Inaugural Address on March 4, 1865, Abraham Lincoln expressed his hope that the end of the war would mean "malice toward none, with charity for all."

A month later, on April 9, 1865, Union General Ulysses S. Grant and Confederate General Robert E. Lee met in Virginia to set the terms of surrender by the South. Both men shared the hope that the surrender would begin a healing for the country.

More American men died in the Civil War—more than 620,000—than in any other war in which Americans fought, before or since. Including those wounded, at least one million men suffered casualties of war in a country of thirty-three million people.

Tracking down all the details about the experiences of the people in this book was not always possible. We read diaries, letters, interviews, and newspaper articles, as well as books written by historians who spent years researching the past, to create the most accurate picture. Some individuals' lives were better documented than others'. Eugenia Phillips left a detailed account of her time before and on Ship Island, including her thoughts and feelings. The Battle of Mobile Bay was documented by Farragut. Numerous reporters covered Lincoln's inauguration. The meeting between Ulysses S. Grant and Robert E. Lee was documented by the generals themselves and by two Union officers who were present.

We compared various sources to create the most truthful account of each event. In some instances, where we could not find every detail, we fictionalized some details, based on historical research. In the Acknowledgments section, you can see our research sources and what has been fictionalized.

You will notice that when we refer to the men in this book, we usually call them by their last names. When we refer to the women, we call them by their first names although, in the era of the Civil War, married women were addressed as Mrs., even by their husbands at times. We found that calling them "Mrs." kept the women from "coming alive" in the stories. In addition, the events involving Julia Ward Howe and Eugenia Phillips also involve their husbands, and it became confusing to call the women and men by their last names. For these reasons, we decided to call all the women in this book by their first names.

THE START OF THE WAR

In the mid 1800s, twenty-two million people lived in the North and South. Of the eleven million inhabitants of the South, four million were slaves.

Life in the North and in the South was very different. The North was a manufacturing center. The South was agricultural. Northerners wanted tariffs, or fees, placed on imported goods. Southerners depended on manufactured goods from England. They didn't want tariffs, because the fees raised the prices of these imported goods. Southerners no longer wanted the federal government telling them what to do; they favored states' rights over federal control.

Although the war did not start over slavery, even before the fighting, the issue divided Americans in the North and the South. The question of ending slavery took on momentum as the war continued. At the time of Lincoln's election in 1860, few political leaders in the North advocated an end to slavery. Lincoln was against slavery, but as late as July 1861 he promised to allow it to continue where it existed, but not allow its expansion into other states. Still, the president's Republican Party was very unpopular in the South.

The tensions and differences finally erupted when South Carolina seceded from the Union on December 20, 1860. Then on April 12 and 13, 1861, rebel Confederates bombarded federal Fort Sumter, and the Civil War began.

Northerners expected to win the war quickly. They had better weapons and equipment, and factories to manufacture more of both. Southerners thought they would win. They believed their men were better shooters, fighters, and horsemen. They also had the advantage of fighting on home territory as most of the battles took place in the South.

July 21, 1861, was a hot, humid day. Lighthearted Washingtonians in carriages traveled twenty-eight miles across the Potomac and into Virginia to picnic. They expected to see the Union army roust the Confederate troops at Bull Run. The small creek at Bull Run flowed down to the town of Manassas Junction. This crucial railroad junction connected two railroad lines, one from Washington and the valley of Virginia north of Manassas, and another that ran south to Richmond. Whichever side controlled this crossing controlled the approach to the Confederate capital in Richmond. The North expected to win that day, march on to capture Richmond, and end the war. But the Union suffered a surprise defeat in what the North ultimately called the First Battle of Bull Run. The

Confederacy named this battle the First Battle of Manassas. Southern women living in the nation's capital were thought to have passed information to the Confederate army about the Union's battle strategy, and a handful were arrested.

The Union regrouped its army. In November 1861 Northerners again packed picnic hampers and traveled across the Potomac River from the capital to see the newly trained troops drill.

"The Battle Hymn of the Republic":
JULIA WARD HOWE

After losing at Bull Run, the Union increased the size and discipline of its armies. President Lincoln named thirty-five-year-old General George B. McClellan Commander of the Grand Army of the Potomac. McClellan assembled 150,000 soldiers around Washington and on the banks of the Potomac River to protect the capital against the Confederate forces camped all around. By October the Confederate flag flew in view of the capital, less than ten miles away. Confederate ships blockaded the river, keeping supplies out of the city.

In November Lincoln put McClellan in charge of all Union forces. The North was impatient for a victory, but McClellan believed the army wasn't ready. He continued drilling the troops and invited dignitaries and the public to watch these "grand reviews." On November 18 the sightseers at Bailey's Crossroads near Munson's Hill in Virginia included the poet Julia Ward Howe, well respected in her hometown of Boston as a literary scholar.

4

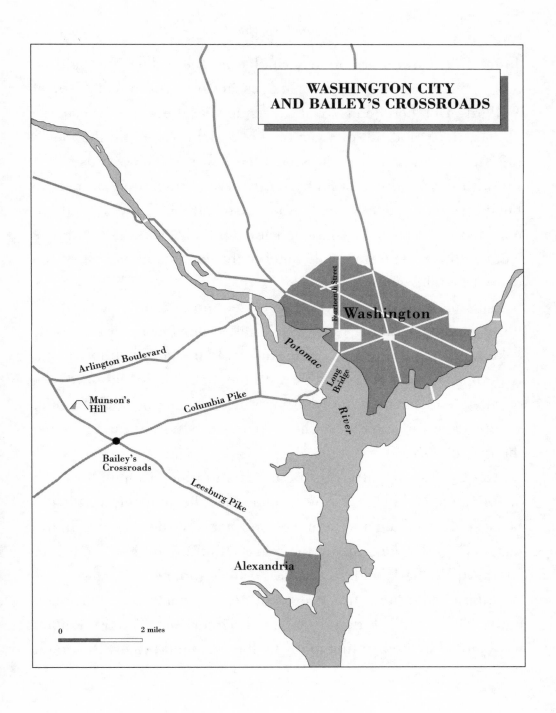

WASHINGTON CITY AND BAILEY'S CROSSROADS

Fourteenth Street

Washington

Potomac

Long Bridge

River

Arlington Boulevard

Munson's Hill

Columbia Pike

Bailey's Crossroads

Leesburg Pike

Alexandria

0   2 miles

Julia Ward Howe's crinolines crinkled as she walked through the lobby. She was dressed in black, as always. The street level of Willard's Hotel on Pennsylvania Avenue near the White House was already noisy and full of cigar smoke at eight o'clock in the morning. Congress would be in session later. Lawmakers were busy talking with the hundreds of lobbyists: Everyone from army officers to businessmen to state officials wanted something. They wanted job commissions or new legislation. They did their business four times a day in this most fashionable hotel in the capital and ate big meals every time they gathered.

This morning Julia smelled sausage, apples, and biscuits from the gentlemen's dining room. She'd taken her meal of wheat pancakes and cream with Eliza Jane Andrew in the ladies' dining room. No proper woman ate in public with the men. There were two sets of rules, one for men and one for women. Her husband, Samuel Gridley Howe—known as Chev—believed strongly in this, even though Julia didn't.

Chev was an officer for the Sanitation Commission in Washington. He'd been in the capital since the summer, working to boost soldier morale and improve conditions for the wounded in the hospitals. Julia had taken their six children to their house in Newport, Rhode Island, to escape Boston's summer.

Julia's white lace cuffs provided the only contrast to her black outfit. Eliza Jane's skirts presented a brighter note. The two women were joined in the bustling lobby by their menfolk. Chev, Reverend

Mr. James Freeman Clarke, and Governor John A. Andrew of Massachusetts all wore military cloaks and high silk hats. Governor Andrew's white kid gloves were impeccable.

Andrew was an avid recruiter for the Union army. Julia couldn't imagine a better war governor. Clarke was Julia's minister at the Unitarian Church of the Disciples in Boston. Everyone in their party was a strong Union supporter and abolitionist.

Julia exited through the door on Fourteenth Street. The city outside was just as busy and noisy as the hotel. The party's coachman was waiting to take them to the grand review. A porter lifted the wicker hamper onto the carriage with their picnic lunch, prepared by the hotel's kitchen.

Julia, who had been in the finest cities and hotels of Europe, was horrified by the look of the capital. It was more of a village than a city. Its wide streets were unpaved. The federal buildings were not yet finished. The Capitol was without a dome.

Their carriage joined other horse-drawn vehicles maneuvering down the rutted street. Each party had received an invitation from General McClellan to attend today's review of the Grand Army of the Potomac. Julia knew the event would be spectacular.

Clusters of brown tents caught the poet's eye as the procession of carriages careened toward the river. The wounded soldiers lying on stretchers or on the bare ground saddened her. She had seen the amputation tables in military hospitals. Her heart broke now at the sight of the many men who had lost their limbs. Their battle wounds had stopped their blood flow and caused gangrene to set in, which made amputation necessary.

Small detachments of the Union army marched past her carriage. The troops want to demonstrate how well they march, she thought. As though to prove her correct, some soldiers saluted.

At the end of Fourteenth Street, the horses' hooves clomped onto the packed dirt roadbed of Long Bridge. Armed federal troops on horseback guarded the bridge, which connected the capital to Virginia. The coachman had said the trip to Bailey's Crossroads near Munson's Hill was seven and a half miles. The rutted dirt roads made travel painfully slow. Julia expected it would take nearly two and a half hours.

Two days ago she had visited the White House, accompanied by Mr. Clarke and Governor and Mrs. Andrew. Mr. Lincoln had sat beneath Gilbert Stuart's portrait of George Washington in the drawing room. How serene Mr. Washington looked. Lines of worry accentuated Mr. Lincoln's cheeks and brow. The only hint of peace in Lincoln's face was in the deep blue of his eyes.

The carriages bumped along the muddy forest road. Julia wondered how many roads wound in and out of the forest and whether they were safe. Confederate soldiers might be hiding up among the trees. She consoled herself with the fact that numerous Union army campgrounds were scattered throughout the two hundred acres around Bailey's Crossroads.

She recalled the stories she'd read about the "Quaker guns" that the Confederate soldiers had left behind at Munson's Hill. The guns were actually logs painted black to look like cannons and fool federal commanders. Northern newspapers had made great fun of the trick. The joke was told at the expense of the Quakers, who were pacifists and supposedly would not go to war. But in fact hundreds of Quakers had taken up arms for the Union.

Finally they arrived at the parade grounds. Julia was glad to leave the carriage and stretch. All about her, men and women dressed in fine clothing spread quilts on the ground. Corks popped. Wineglasses clinked. Silver utensils caught the light. Julia opened their food hamper. It was a feast—boiled poultry, ham, tongue, and rice garnished with sweetbreads and parsley. Then she saw the bread pudding, her favorite. Amid the merriment, small orchestras began playing. The strains of violins comforted her, but it still felt eerie here. The pine and oak trees of the surrounding hills seemed to swallow up the visitors.

At about two o'clock soldiers in blue uniforms and overcoats assembled in columns on the muddy plateau. The sight of tens of thousands of men and their crisp and colorful regimental flags caught Julia's breath. There were more soldiers bearing arms, heads held high, than she had ever imagined. The orchestras stopped playing. The silence was awe-inspiring.

Then the commanders called out maneuvers. "Attention! Bayonets fixed! Advance!" Columns of soldiers marched in unison. Their movements were precise and perfect. So many boots changing step

made hollow, sucking sounds in the mud. Muskets clicked and glittered in the afternoon sunlight. Julia heard someone say, "They march like the lords of the world." She agreed.

The cannons rolled in. Their metal shone brilliantly in the sunlight. The black Parrott guns, named for a French inventor, followed in a long line like big, ugly crustaceans. Next were the cavalrymen on their fine horses. It was hard not to be taken in at this moment by the allure of war. In principle, Julia was against war, except to rid the nation of slavery.

Silence fell as McClellan appeared on horseback. The hundreds of spectators clapped and shouted enthusiastically. He was shorter in his saddle than the others, but his presence was monumental. Julia's eyes filled with tears.

With a dramatic sweep of his sword, the young commander called his troops to order. Julia tried to relax and settle in for the show. Trumpets blared the opening notes of a march, and McClellan and his officers rode their majestic horses through the ranks of soldiers. The soldiers held their formal salute until he finished inspecting them. Had she ever seen anything this impressive?

McClellan took the position of honor on the reviewing stand with his top officers. The brigades left the columns to demonstrate their fine marching to him.

"Company advance! Flags unfurl!"

For the next hour the regiments marched. The soldiers, waiting their turns on the plateau, never faltered in posture.

Suddenly gunshots sounded from the woods. McClellan moved his sword in an abrupt sweep, signaling the troops to disperse. As unexpected as the enemy gunfire was the rapid end to the music. Julia and Eliza Jane ran for their carriage as their men saw to the belongings. Hundreds of spectators fought for the same path to safety. People screamed and scurried to waiting carriages. The horses reared from the excitement. Julia's coachman pulled back on the reins.

She hurriedly stepped into the carriage. No time to settle her skirts. She felt Eliza Jane push against her. The men tumbled into the vehicle. Their carriage joined many others as the driver struggled to file out onto the solitary road away from Munson's Hill. Julia heard shots nearby. Her heart felt as if it would explode from her chest.

"It's only a Confederate skirmish, a nuisance attack by a small force," Governor Andrew informed them.

Julia turned and saw Union soldiers with guns drawn in firing position. They had rushed to protect their comrades in the grand review against an enemy ambush. Some soldiers were in defensive positions. This *was* war. Many Union regiments were scrambling a helter-skelter retreat from Munson's Hill down the same road as the carriages!

Some of the troops began to sing:

"John Brown's body lies a-mouldering in the ground;
John Brown's body lies a-mouldering in the grave;
And his soul goes marching on.
Glory, glory, hallelujah,
Glory, glory, hallelujah,
His soul goes marching on."

The loud strains of this popular Union army song raised Julia's spirits. She was grateful to abolitionist John Brown for trying to keep slavery out of the territory of Kansas. But his revolt of slaves at Harpers Ferry, Virginia, had been ill-conceived. Because of it, he came to an unfortunate end. Julia had seen his wife when Mrs. Brown went to visit her husband in prison before he was hanged. She admired the woman's strength.

Julia sang the second verse along with the soldiers:

"He's gone to be a soldier in the Army of the Lord,
He's gone to be a soldier in the Army of the Lord,
His soul goes marching on."

A soldier saluted her.

"Can't you write some good words for that stirring tune?" James Freeman Clarke asked.

Julia didn't respond.

The carriage continued along the bumpy road. The numbers of troops on the road thinned as companies of soldiers departed for their camps. The sky darkened as evening approached. The carriages and soldiers were guided by the campfires all along the way. Melodies from tin whistles blended with the night sounds from the woods and soothed Julia's nerves. Wild turkeys gobbled and owls shrieked as they passed. Finally Julia's carriage arrived at Long Bridge. Her driver received a nod from the guards to cross.

Back at Willard's, she noted the trip to the city had taken more than three hours. She decided against her nightly visit to the hotel salon on the main level. She was a regular and popular visitor there and enjoyed the conversations about literature or the evils of slavery. But she felt too tired to join in tonight. She bade good night to her husband and walked through the cigar smoke in the lobby up to her room.

She undressed to the cadence of the troops marching below the hotel window and the sirens of the ambulances rushing about the city. She placed her head on the pillow, said a prayer for her six children, and closed her eyes. The smoke of the campfires still hung in her imaginiation. The trumpet music replayed in her ears.

She awoke near dawn and rushed to the desk in her hotel room. Her poems often needed to be written in the quiet of the early dawn.

She usually counted syllables and was meticulous about rhyme scheme. But this morning the words to her poem almost wrote themselves. She could hardly see what she penned in the poor light, but it didn't matter. The melody of "John Brown's Body" guided her as she wrote new verses. The day at the camp, the soldiers, their discipline—all had inspired her. Her belief that right would triumph was guiding her now. God was with the Union. Her poem felt like a revelation. She wrote:

> *"Mine eyes have seen the glory of the coming of the Lord:*
>   *He is trampling out the wine-press where the grapes of*
>   *wrath are stored;*
>   *He hath loosed the fateful lightnings of his terrible swift*
>   *sword:*
>   *His truth is marching on. . . . "*

* * *

Julia Ward Howe's poem was published as "The Battle Hymn of the Republic" in February 1862 by The Atlantic Monthly *magazine. She received five dollars in payment. A comparison of her original words and the final version shows she made thirteen minor changes. In the story we have used her original version. The complete text on pages 109–110 includes all her changes.*

This poem was not her first work in print for The Atlantic Monthly. *She had written travel letters for it since 1859. Julia was prolific, but most of her writing was unpublished. Among her published works is* Passion Flowers, *a collection of poems. She also wrote literary criticism and a novel, which she never finished.*

Julia was born Julia Ward in 1819 in New York and was tutored at home and in private schools. She received three honorary college degrees, including one from Smith College. As she matured, she became a believer in women's rights. In 1868 she was elected the first president of the New England Woman Suffrage Association. She became a Unitarian in her later years.

The first public singing of "The Battle Hymn of the Republic" was in Framingham, Massachusetts, in 1862 in honor of George Washington's birthday. President Lincoln heard it after the Battle of Gettysburg. Julia herself was invited to read the poem publicly on many occasions where she was honored by the great minds of her time, including Ralph Waldo Emerson.

The Massachusetts Thirtieth Infantry Band sang the hymn at Julia's funeral in 1910. By that time many in America had taken to comparing her fondly to Queen Victoria. She had become the "Queen of America."

"In Good Spirits":
EUGENIA PHILLIPS

On August 23, 1861, Eugenia Phillips, along with two of her daughters and her sister, was arrested as a spy in the Union capital. The women were accused of passing information about Union strategy for the Battle of Bull Run (Manassas) to the Confederate army. When no proof confirmed the charge, they were released. Fearing continued harassment, the family moved to New Orleans, believing it to be safe. They were wrong. On April 25, 1862, this Southern city was captured in a daring naval attack by David Glasgow Farragut. The Confederate Stars and Bars flag was hauled down and replaced with the Stars and Stripes.

Union Major General Benjamin Franklin Butler was put in charge of the city on May 1, 1862. He faced severe opposition from the city's residents, especially the women. They shouted insults to Yankee soldiers. They wore the forbidden colors of the Confederate flag and sang Confederate songs. Butler issued an order stating that

17

any woman found "by word, gesture or movement, to insult or to show contempt for any officer or soldier would be treated . . . as an indecent woman of the streets." Punishment would be imprisonment. The people of New Orleans were outraged.

* * *

"Gobble, gobble!" shouted Emma, Eugenia Phillips's eleven-year-old daughter.

Emma chased her friends around the patio. Her brothers, nine-year-old William and seven-year-old Philip Lee, screamed the loudest and ran the fastest. Everyone was pretending to be rats. Emma was the rat catcher. For the last few days, all Eugenia's youngest three did was imitate the "Man Eating Rats." Of all the magic lantern stories, this one was their favorite. Eugenia was delighted to see them running and laughing so freely. Tonight all seemed beautiful on Bourbon Street in the French Quarter. But life in New Orleans was not normal. With Benjamin Butler now in command, no one was safe. Eugenia kept her doors and shutters closed and her seven children indoors as much as possible.

Butler frequently sent his soldiers unannounced to search for weapons. A few nights ago, they had ransacked a neighbor's house. No weapons had been found. They rarely were during such searches, but valuable silver often disappeared and ended up in the dining rooms of wealthy Northerners. One of Butler's many nick-names was "Spoons." Eugenia had given her own silver to the

English consul in New Orleans for safekeeping.

Any public display of Confederate sentiment met with retaliation. Butler hoisted the U.S. flag above the Mint. William B. Mumford took it down. Butler arrested him. Five days later Butler ordered Mumford hanged without a trial. Eugenia did not have great respect for Mumford. He was a gambler, not a gentleman, but that was no excuse to hang him without allowing him a lawyer. Butler's brutality sickened her. She was outraged, but powerless. She did what little she could. She led a drive to collect money for Mrs. Mumford and her children. She had heard rumors that her action infuriated Butler. Be that as it may, she felt it had been the right thing to do.

"Rat catcher!" Emma shouted.

The children chanted the phrase over and over. The hot, moist air and the closeness of so many people made Eugenia giddy. Her husband, Philip, filled the magic lantern's oil lamp. He lit the wick and adjusted the flame. Immediately the image of a huge sleeping man wearing his nightcap appeared on the courtyard wall.

"Gobble, gobble!" Emma cried. Children and adults alike booed, hissed, and shouted, "Gobble, gobble."

The owner of the magic lantern started moving a piece of glass up and down on the slides, and the old man's mouth began to open and close, as if he was breathing heavily or snoring. The children made snoring sounds in rhythm with the movement of the man's mouth.

Then the owner turned the crank on the slide that rotated another piece of glass. Suddenly rat after rat leaped onto the bed and headed straight for the old man's mouth. The children screamed as the old man chewed and swallowed the rats.

"Again! Again!" The children shrieked until the unexpected sound of muffled drums and horses' hooves on the cobblestone street stifled their merriment.

"Maybe it's the Beast!" Emma shouted. Philip Lee laughed at one of Butler's nicknames.

"Shh, I've told you not to say that," Eugenia scolded her daughter. Butler surely deserved the nickname, but she had to teach the children caution. She pulled Philip Lee toward her. On a recent walk through town, Philip Lee had spat at soldiers. Eugenia and Philip punished him and repeatedly explained the seriousness of his action. They formally apologized to Butler and acknowledged their son's wrong behavior. But Butler accepted no excuses, even for a seven-year-old.

Everyone moved closer to the street for a better look. It was a funeral procession. Behind the honor guard was a wagon with a casket draped with the Union flag. A row of carriages followed. Eugenia assumed this was the funeral of the Yankee lieutenant George De Kay. She had read about his death in the morning newspaper.

From neighboring houses people spilled onto Bourbon Street. Many wore the forbidden Confederate colors. Eugenia scanned the passing carriages. Twenty in all. Most were empty. A ridiculous, flamboyant gesture, she thought. Especially in the French Quarter, where funerals of wealthy Creoles were usually gala parties to send off the soul of the departed.

"Gobble, gobble," Emma chanted.

Eugenia couldn't help but laugh at her daughter's silliness.

"Let's go to Christ's Church," someone said. "The funeral service is being held there."

Philip Lee pulled at her skirt, signaling his desire to go. She ignored him and led her children away from the gate, back to the safety of their home. Her family was Jewish. She had never been to Christ's Church. She was not about to go tonight of all nights.

On Monday morning her three youngest children were in her sitting room. Eugenia felt a quiet that she hadn't felt for weeks. Perhaps life would be easier from now on.

At ten o'clock there was a furious ringing of the doorbell. Probably business for Philip. He was already at work. Her servant would take care of it. A few minutes later, the servant rushed up the stairs to her room. "Missus, a Yankee soldier here to see you."

"Ask him to leave his message, please."

"He says he will not deliver it to anyone but Mrs. Phillips."

Emma began crying. Philip Lee clung to her skirt. "It's a mistake," Eugenia said, trying to calm them. William raced after her as she started down the stairs. She grabbed him just in time to send him back upstairs. Her knees were trembling. She had to keep calm. The children had seen her arrested in the capital; she didn't want them upset again. She walked slowly down the stairs.

An armed soldier was seated in the hall. How dare he take such liberties in her home! He thrust a piece of paper at her. She recognized Benjamin Butler's seal. Slowly she slipped a finger under the wax seal. She needed time to cool her anger. The curt note read: "Bring me Mrs. Phillips."

"This is a mistake. It cannot be for me," she said quietly to the soldier.

What reason could Butler have to send for her? Were the rumors true? Could he be angry that she had collected money for Mrs. Mumford? Surely that was not a crime. She had read in the newspaper that the crowd at the Yankee officer's funeral was so disruptive, the service had to be stopped. But she had not gone there, so he couldn't be angry about that. However, she had no choice but to go to him. She could not disobey a military order. She sent a servant to tell Philip to meet her there.

Philip was waiting for her at Butler's headquarters. The officer led them through rooms filled with men and women, black and white.

"Where is Mrs. Phillips?" She recognized Butler's voice booming from behind a green door. The soldier informed Philip that he could not go with Eugenia.

Impossible! She would not greet this beast without Philip. She defiantly plopped on a seat outside Butler's office. "You can get a rope and drag me by force there, for if my husband is not allowed to be with me, I shall not move," she said.

The officer greeted her words with silence and disappeared behind the green door.

He returned and escorted Eugenia and Philip into Benjamin Butler's office. Butler was sitting at a desk on a platform. Members of his staff were seated along the walls. Butler's face was crimson with anger. Eugenia felt no fear, only outrage, for she had done nothing wrong.

Butler bellowed, "You were seen on your patio laughing at the remains of a Yankee officer."

How did he know that she had laughed? He hadn't been there. Who had told him? Had one of his officers recognized her? No matter. He would never believe the truth—that she had been laughing at Emma's comment—so why bother telling him? She looked him in the eye and spoke not a word.

"Do you have anything to say in your defense, Mrs. Phillips?" Butler asked.

"I was in good spirits on Saturday," she answered.

Butler glared. "I do not call you a vulgar woman such as those who wear Confederate colors and empty their chamber pots in the street. I call you an uncommonly vulgar woman. I sentence you indefinitely to prison on Ship Island. And you shall have no verbal or written communication with anyone there."

"General Butler, I shall not allow such language to my wife," protested Philip. Philip had met Benjamin Butler on a number of occasions. Their conversation had been civil if not pleasant.

Butler gripped the pistol on his desk. "Gag that man. Put him in prison."

Eugenia swallowed the fire in her throat and took her husband's arm. "Leave this to me," she whispered. I can handle Benjamin Butler, and I will endure Ship Island, too, she resolved. She knew it would not be easy. Ship Island was the dumping ground for suspected spies, parole violators, prisoners of war, pro-Confederate sympathizers, and Union soldiers who committed crimes.

Butler snatched a piece of paper and slowly began writing. She watched his hand deliberately form each letter. He was writing out her sentence slowly, hoping she would throw herself on his mercy and beg his pardon. No, she would never do that. He had charged her and sentenced her without judge or jury. He was a brute, but she would meet his outrageous punishment with dignity and silence.

Two days later, at eight in the morning, Eugenia was taken to the dock at Lake Pontchartrain to board a boat to Ship Island. Phoebe Dunlap, Eugenia's Irish maid, who had been with her for fifteen years, was at her side. Phoebe had offered to come with her. Butler had agreed.

Philip was there to say good-bye. Eugenia saw how sad he looked. She had to make him smile before she could leave.

"Am I not lucky to have a summer retreat when you are to remain in New Orleans?" she said to Philip in earshot of Union soldiers. His sad face brightened at her animated remark.

She turned to walk toward the boat and was overcome with emotion to see twenty of the city's most aged and respected citizens. They had come despite Butler's rule against crowds. They were risking imprisonment, for everyone thought that Butler was crazy enough to arrest them, too, if he so chose.

An officer read the official charges: "Mrs. Phillips, wife of Philip Phillips, had been imprisoned for her traitorous proclivities and acts in the Union capital, but was released. In New Orleans she trained her children to spit upon Union officers. Their child and she and her husband apologized for that act and were again forgiven. But she was found, during the funeral procession of Lieutenant De Kay, laughing and mocking at his remains. Asked if this were so, she contemptuously replied, 'I was in good spirits that day.' She is to be banished to Ship Island in the state of Mississippi for an indefinite period of time."

People bowed their heads in a silent ovation to her. They knew how difficult her life would now be. She would eat what other prisoners there ate. She would be allowed mail from her family but denied any written or oral communication with anyone else.

Eugenia lifted her skirt and stepped into the boat. Phoebe followed. The two women huddled next to each other in a cabin, surrounded by Yankee soldiers. Everything about these men was filthy—their clothing, their shoes, their dirt-encrusted nails. They reeked of whiskey and sweat.

The boat pulled away from the shore. The men laughed and

boasted about their latest drunken brawls. They used words that were never spoken around ladies. But what did they care about ladies? They were not gentlemen.

She would not let on how sickened she was by their coarse words. To drown out their crude language, she asked Phoebe to read to her. But there was no relief from the soldiers' ugly talk. When she could no longer bear it, she swallowed her pride and asked the captain for a private place for her and Phoebe to sit. He refused.

Ship Island was sixty miles from New Orleans. The sun beat down unmercifully on the cabin. Perspiration drenched her blouse and undergarments. Her throat became parched. No one brought her even a sip of water, and she refused to ask. The wind picked up some, and the constant rocking of the boat turned her stomach. I must not be sick in front of these men. She willed herself to remain calm. She would never complain, no matter what happened. She would never give the Yankees the satisfaction.

Eugenia had heard that the island was a narrow sandbar, seven miles long and one half mile wide. Most of the island was supposed to be barren, but when the boat docked, she saw a cluster of buildings. She felt hopeful. One of these might be her living quarters. Perhaps life here would not be as bad as she feared.

The soldiers left the boat. Phoebe and Eugenia sat and waited for someone to come. Finally a young man, who introduced himself as Captain George Blodgett, greeted them. He helped them out of the boat. Eugenia found herself up to her ankles in deep, scorching sand. Suddenly she clutched her stomach and doubled over in pain. She suppressed a scream.

The captain had no idea why she was sick. When told that she had eaten nothing, he hurried off to get her some brandy to settle her stomach.

Blodgett led them far away from the clusters of buildings to a barren stretch of sand dunes on the western tip of the island. There was not a tree or blade of grass anywhere. Perched on a dune was an old railroad passenger car. It looked like a big box with one window and a small door hung on leather straps. There was not even a curve on the flat tin roof to keep off the sun.

Humid, fetid air filled her nostrils when Blodgett opened the door. She stared at a chamber pot and large piles of dirt on the broken wooden floor. Filth and dust were everywhere. Not a sign of comfort. No table. No chair. No bed. She noticed an iron ring on the wall. A torturing device, no doubt. Some poor captured Confederate soldier had probably been here before.

Mosquitoes swarmed about her. How would she get rid of these bloodthirsty insects? She had vowed never to complain, no matter what, but the words slipped out of her mouth. "I want to live for my husband and my children. But I will go wild if I remain here all night to be bitten to death."

Blodgett left abruptly. He returned with a piece of netting, hung it over a nail, and stretched it across part of the floor. Then he left.

Suddenly her face felt cold. Ridiculous! It was steaming inside these four walls. How would she survive? And poor Phoebe. If Eugenia had known it would be this horrible, she never would have let her come. But who could have imagined any man would treat women this way?

She expected Blodgett to return with food. She knew the law. Prisoners of war were to be fed. She would receive the same rations as the soldiers. An hour passed. Two hours. She knew then that there would be no food tonight. When she could no longer bear the suffocating heat, she and Phoebe curled up on the dirty floor under the netting. What would the next day bring? she fretted. Exhaustion triumphed, and she fell asleep almost immediately.

Neither food nor water arrived the next morning. Every part of her body felt sticky and dirty. In all her life, she had never been unwashed or unfed. Would anyone ever come to help them? Footsteps outside. She peeked out the window. A guard was marching back and forth. Maybe he would help. She called out, asking permission to buy a loaf of bread or some crackers. She had no sooner spoken than someone thrust his arms into the window and started cursing her. She turned away. Silence.

An hour later Captain Blodgett appeared. "Well, Mrs. Phillips, I hope you have been attended to." When she told him what had happened, he exclaimed, "Good God, can such things be?"

Even he is shocked, she thought. He left quickly. She expected him to come back with food, but he did not return.

An hour after that, a note arrived. George Avery, a doctor on the island, had learned of her situation and offered to help. Soon tea and toast were brought to her and Phoebe. Eugenia was touched by the doctor's kindness. She feared he might be punished for writing to her, for it was against the rules. If only she could thank him, tell him how comforting his kindness felt.

The door burst open. A tall man with a nasty grimace rushed toward her, almost striking her in the face with his fist. "If you ever again communicate with anyone on the island, I will hang you up by your legs," he ranted.

She was speechless and horrified. Someone had reported the doctor's kindness. She knew that this brute, who didn't introduce himself, was probably General Neal Dow, the commander of the island. He would probably punish the good doctor. Dow stormed out of her prison. Again, only silence and hot, dank air.

That evening two hands reached through the window, with two tin pans. Then the hands passed in two spoons and cups; then a tray with dinner. She smelled rancid bacon. Bits of it had been cooked with crackers and rice. Four biscuits were on the tray. She touched them. They were hard and stale. She looked into the cup. What was this masquerading as tea? But she ate, because she was starved. Phoebe ate too.

After dinner Eugenia called the guard and asked for a broom. "I cannot live in this filth," she explained. "Denied," he snapped. Obviously Butler had given orders to make her life as unpleasant as possible. She would not let them break her will, no matter what.

And more important, she would not let Philip find out how she was being treated. It would pain him that he was powerless to change it.

A month passed. There was no relief from the suffocating summer heat. No relief from the boredom but the few books and sewing she was allowed to have. Then one day a soldier told her that she and Phoebe would be moving to new lodgings. She tried not to laugh when she saw what he described as "better housing." Better housing, indeed. It was a boarded-up building nearer the officers' headquarters. She tried to focus on the positives. It was cleaner than the other building. And now she had a chair and table and a bed with a mattress. She was also closer to the other prisoners. She wasn't allowed to speak to any of them, nor were they allowed to speak to her. Nonetheless, being closer to them felt strangely comforting.

The summer storms came. The roof leaked. Water constantly washed into the building and soaked their bedding and clothes. The same inedible food arrived three times a day. She ate to survive. Too often she could not swallow what was served. She did not have to look down at her baggy clothing to know how much weight she had lost. She was not allowed outside for exercise and fresh air. And with greater cruelty, neither was Phoebe. Eugenia's brain felt as barren as the island. She had read the books she brought with her many times over.

Her only consolation was the weekly mail from home. She answered the letters as lightheartedly as she could. She was certain all her mail—incoming and outgoing—was read. She would not let any Yankee, especially Benjamin Butler, see that her spirits had been weakened.

> *August 9, 1862*
>
> *Dear Philip:*
>
> *I am forbidden all communication. But seclusion brings reflection. During the lovely, calm nights, at all hours I am up and communing with the beautiful stars and generous moon. Both whisper to me the secrets of others and tell me to look at the man in the moon and consider the spots in the sun, for between these two is there to be found one good, honest, just man.*
>
> *My sister tells me that you no longer take the air on the "Patio." Good. I approve of this. That "Patio" belongs to history and should not be profaned.*
>
> *Some good soul has sent in a melon, so goodbye to philosophy.*

Eugenia's health weakened. She had headaches and severe pain in her muscles and joints. A doctor prescribed "perfect quiet" and arrowroot. She swallowed her pride and begged an officer for some boiled water to mix with arrowroot. He agreed, but only if he could find a spare soldier to boil the water. Eugenia knew he would never return. She asked Phoebe to heat water over a candle.

The next morning the cadenced count of soldiers drilling outside her prison awakened her. Marching, shouting, loud commands. It had to be deliberate, another cruel blow aimed at her, for certainly this was not the "perfect quiet" prescribed by the doctor.

Her body desperately needed nourishment—an egg, a piece of fresh fruit, some fish. She asked to buy an egg. The request was refused. She asked for Phoebe to be allowed into the kitchen to make her something. That request was refused. The days dragged by.

Finally Butler gave permission for her to go to New Orleans "on parole" for treatment. She refused. She had done nothing wrong to need parole from him. She would show Butler her strength under these atrocious circumstances. She would have liberty or nothing.

Earlier, on August 6, Anna La Rue, who had been imprisoned for having dressed in Confederate colors with a secession badge, was released. When she passed by Eugenia's window, Eugenia called after her: "Tell General Butler I am still in good spirits."

September came. She feared she could not last through the cold and damp of winter. Still she wrote not a word about her troubles to her children. In her daily letters to them, she invented happy stories, hoping they would believe them.

September 1, 1862

My darling little Boys and little Emma,
Dear Mother never allows a day to pass without thinking of all her loved little ones and a night to arrive

without praying to God to keep you all well and make good, obedient children of you all.

I would like you to see the great big gun boats the Yankees have here. They look fine sailing around. And when the sea is rough I watch them rolling from one side to the other. The sailors make a great noise when they land in boatloads to bathe. They play like little boys and are full of fun.

The soldiers are very good and kind.

Despite what she wrote to her family, she knew she had to get off the island soon or she would die. She wrote to Philip, asking him to remember her kindly to Reverdy Johnson, who had been appointed by President Lincoln to investigate Butler's activities in New Orleans. Perhaps Johnson could help secure her release.

On September 11 an officer pushed a bundle of papers at her. Another order for further atrocities, she thought. She pushed the papers away.

"You must read it," he said. "It's all right." There was an unexpected gentleness in his voice.

She opened the papers and read: "Mrs. Phillips, confined at Ship Island, is hereby released."

She gasped, and then found it hard to breathe. She had been in this horrible place for more than two months. Now she and Phoebe were free. She was going home without having apologized to

Benjamin Butler. She had triumphed.

* * *

When Eugenia appeared at the door of her home, she was so pale and thin that her servant thought she was a ghost. When she saw her children, she screamed and then fainted. Weeks passed before she felt calm.

Immediately after her release, Eugenia's husband, Philip, worked to get his family out of New Orleans. On October 29 they left in a small schooner filled with other Southerners. They settled in LaGrange, Georgia, and bought a farm. Philip practiced law. A hospital was opened in the village, and Eugenia was placed in charge. She and her older daughters devoted themselves to caring for wounded Confederate soldiers. Eventually three thousand citizens of New Orleans who refused to take the pledge of loyalty were expelled from the city. Benjamin Butler, who had aroused much attention for his cruel measures, was removed from his New Orleans command by President Lincoln on December 23, 1862.

Years after Philip's death, Eugenia lived again in Washington. She met Benjamin Butler at social occasions. It is documented that she nodded but said nothing when she saw him.

The patio that Eugenia referred to in her letter was the patio that she and her family had been on when the funeral parade passed.

MARY JACKSON

Two years after the war began, the Confederate army desperately needed food. So did civilians. Southern farmers could not grow enough for the population. It was impossible for the railroad to bring in enough to feed the army and the swelling number of people in the crowded cities, especially the capital city of Richmond, Virginia. With food scarce, prices soared.

In March 1863, Confederate President Jefferson Davis ordered farmers to sell their crops to the army at half price. That same month women, anxious about feeding their families, rioted in Atlanta, Georgia; Salisbury, North Carolina; Mobile, Alabama; and Petersburg, Virginia. Hoping to calm things down, Davis proclaimed March 27 a day of prayer and fasting.

The scarcities continued, and food prices did not drop. Southern women remained angry. On April 1, shopkeeper Mary Jackson organized a meeting at Belvidere Hill Baptist Church in Richmond's west end working-class neighborhood of Oregon Hill. Women in and near the city came to discuss the desperate situation.

* * *

Mary Jackson stood in the pulpit and looked out at the three hundred women and girls and two boys in the church. Many there were teenagers. Most of the women were less fortunate than she. Mary and her husband, Elisha, lived on a farm three miles away in Henrico County. Most of the women worked at Tredegar Iron Works. They worked shifts, night and day, to make small arms and ammunition for the army. Every day they breathed in stale factory air and iron dust. No amount of scrubbing could rid their faces of their grayish pallor. Three weeks ago an explosion at the ammunition factory had killed sixty-nine workers. Sixty-two were women.

Mary was glad to see Martha Fergusson. Last night the two women had argued over whether Martha would attend. She wasn't surprised to see wealthy Margaret Pomfrey in her fur shawl. Mrs. Pomfrey had traveled by carriage from her farm in New Kent County, twelve miles away. Mary Johnson had also come. The big-boned, sixty-year-old impatiently raised her fist to signal Jackson to begin.

Mary Jackson took up her silent suggestion. "Let us prepare to confront the merchants tomorrow," she said.

There were cheers and nods of agreement from the tired, tense faces.

Mary continued, "The item of business is the food shortage." She listened attentively as one woman after another described her empty cupboards and her children's grumbling stomachs. The women's voices shook in anger as they out-shouted one another about the high cost of food. Butter was up from its prewar price of 14¢ per pound to $2.85 per pound. A dozen eggs were at an all-time high of $1.50. Many women stated the obvious: Only the rich can afford to eat. Why should the army pay less? There should be one price for all. Our money grows more worthless every day. The Confederate government is at fault.

Mary Jackson's anger was more personal. Her oldest, nineteen-year-old Francis, was in the army. Mary and her husband had tried to obtain his release. Elisha painted houses for a living. They had three other children; the youngest was five. The family desperately needed Francis's labor as help. Their request had been refused.

"Bread or blood!" shouted Mary Johnson, raising her fist high.

"Bread or blood! Bread or blood!" The women chanted the cry that had been used by women in the other Southern cities.

"I move that we send a delegation to make our demands known to the governor," said Martha Fergusson.

Mary Johnson seconded the motion.

Mary Jackson called for a vote. A rush of "ayes" filled the hall. No one asked for a hand count to confirm that the decision was unanimous.

"Very well, but, remember, we mustn't go like a parcel of heathens. We must go quietly into the stores when we demand goods at government prices," Mary Jackson added.

Mary Johnson disagreed. "If they refuse, we shall take the goods by force," she shouted.

Mary Jackson tried to ignore the comment about force. "Now, I need you all to pledge to tell at least one other person about the protest." She pointed out the obvious: The greater their numbers, the better their chance of being taken seriously.

Mary Johnson insisted: "Bring weapons in case persuasion is needed."

"Here's to persuaders," someone shouted. The women stomped their feet and clapped. They now had a name among themselves— "persuaders"—for the hammers, hatchets, axes, knives, and guns they would carry tomorrow.

"Please, for safety's sake, leave the children at home." Mary Jackson was worried about what might happen if the women really brought "persuaders." "We'll meet at my stall at eight tomorrow morning." She adjourned the meeting.

The crowd quieted once outside the church. Women from the neighborhood walked home, talking to one another. Mrs. Pomfrey left in her carriage. Mary climbed into the wagon her husband used for business. She tightened the horse's reins and gave the holler to head for home. The meeting had gone well. She knew what she was doing was right. The soldiers needed to be fed, but so did their families. War demanded sacrifice, and the women of Richmond had sacrificed and suffered much. Many had already lost loved ones in battle. Tomorrow they would protest as women all over the Confederacy were doing.

Thursday, April 2, 1863, dawned a perfect spring day: warm air, sunshine, and the fresh, green smell of rich soil. Not a cloud marred the sky. It was hard to believe that only ten days ago, a foot of snow had blanketed the city.

Mary waved good-bye to her husband and children and plodded down Deep Run Turnpike on foot. Walking was difficult. She had on a simple day dress with a plain, long skirt. A shawl and black bonnet were enough. The snow had melted, making the roads muddy and deeply rutted. Before she reached the half-mile point of the three-mile journey to her stall at the Second Market, the hemline of her skirt hung heavy with mud. Her petticoats and thick stockings were soaked.

She braced herself as she approached Camp Lee and the Old Fairgrounds encampment at Monroe Park. The stench of blood and death choked her. Wounded soldiers were everywhere. Some were being carried into tents. Others lay on stretchers. Richmond's hospitals were overflowing, so doctors examined the wounded wherever they could. Some people had opened their homes as makeshift hospitals. Women in Richmond—white, free blacks, and slaves—tended the wounded. There wasn't enough soap or bandages or drugs. Men with injuries too serious to be treated were left to die wherever they were. She turned her face away. These days the sight

of amputees was all too common. Mary said a quick prayer for
Francis as she walked.

Traffic increased as she neared the market. Liveries opened to
take in horses. The sounds of riders shouting "whoa" and clicking
their reins mixed with the clanking of wagon wheels and the whis-
tle of the train. Ninety thousand people were living here now—more
than three times the number before the war. People swelled the
poorer neighborhoods. There wasn't enough drinking water.
Influenza and cholera were spreading.

Every day more people arrived. Southerners living up North had
moved back to be with their families. People from the countryside
were relocating to the city, thinking they would be safer with the
twenty-five thousand troops stationed here. Thousands more soldiers traipsed through the city daily on their way to the front.

Turning left on Sixth Street off Broad, Mary pulled out her
pocket watch and checked the time. Seven forty-five. Good, she was
early. Second Market was empty except for a few merchants setting
up their stalls. She greeted Robert Redford at his stall on Sixth and
Marshall. She nodded to James Tyler, another shopkeeper. Tyler
was talking to two policemen, Washington Griffin and William
Kelley. Last week Mary Jackson had told Officer Griffin what she
was planning and that she would shoot him if he tried to stop it.

"You're going through with it, Mary?" Tyler called out.

She answered with a nod.

The men snickered and shoved one another in jest. They weren't taking her seriously. Why stop to argue? They'd soon see how serious she was. She grabbed a knife from her stall and wrapped it in paper so she wouldn't hurt herself. She put it in her waist sash. She didn't care if they saw.

She waited impatiently for the women to arrive. Hundreds of them came. And a handful of boys. They crowded the market, heading for her stall. Many women brandished hatchets, knives, and even pistols, without a thought about who might see. She sensed their determination. If the governor didn't agree to help lower prices, they would go on to the stores. They wouldn't be stopped.

At eight o'clock, she burrowed through the crowd to lead them outside. Everyone was talking at once:

"Let's go straight to the stores."

"No, to the governor."

"No, to the stores!"

"No, to the governor!"

The women surged out of the market, upsetting some stalls. Mary had envisioned the group following her, the leader, but this wasn't the case. She crossed Broad Street at Seventh behind scores of women. The crowd swarmed from all directions, toward George Washington's statue at the northwestern section of Capitol Square.

She spotted Martha Fergusson and Mary Johnson. They were leading a delegation toward the Governor's Mansion several hundred feet from Washington's statue. Mary Jackson waited impatiently with the crowd. How would Governor John Lechter respond?

"Bread or blood!" she shouted.

Other women picked up the cry. "Bread or blood!" The roar of the many voices pulsated in Mary's head.

It was but a few minutes until a woman in the delegation ran back with news: The governor was already at work in the Capitol.

The throng rushed forward. The women pushed one another in a crazed frenzy to get to the Capitol. They were out of control. Thankfully, the governor was now on the steps of the Capitol. Mary was relieved the women quieted down to listen to him.

"Ladies," he began.

The women cheered.

"Life is difficult for everyone," he continued. "But this is not the way to solve your problem." His voice was tight. "If you try to force your way into taking any goods, it will be over the point of the bayonet."

Mary turned abruptly from him. How dare he tell them how to behave? She was sure his family had more than enough to eat.

The women responded by rushing out of the square. Their shouts rattled horses traveling down Ninth Street. Some horses stumbled as carts careened and crashed. Women picked up what they wanted from the goods that spilled into the street. Mary rushed into the melee. How had she lost her leadership? She felt the white-hot anger in the air and a thickened sense of purpose. She only hoped this new purpose wasn't sinister.

"Where are you going?" a man shouted from a doorway.

A frail young woman in tattered clothes shouted back, "To get something to eat!"

The crowd moved like a ship on the James River without a navigator. It steered of its own accord, getting more unruly as it hurried down Ninth and across Franklin to Main. Mary followed. She felt she wasn't even in control of her own walking. Still she pressed on as more people filed in from side streets.

The pace quickened. There was an eruption of yelling and cursing and running. The mob splintered into fragments and spilled down intersecting streets.

On Cary Street Mary Jackson ran with others to the warehouse district along the canal. Here were the stores that sold goods to the government. She hurried past the canal basin, pushing and shoving her way forward. At one of the docks, called Shockoe Slip, owners Robert Pollard and Joshua Walker stood in the doorway of their store.

Mary Johnson held her ax high and defiantly led the way toward the two shopkeepers. A throng of women and boys filed in behind her. A young boy flashed his ax.

"We demand that you sell us bacon at a reasonable price," Mary Johnson roared. Thunderous shouts and waving weapons accompanied her demand.

For a brief moment, it seemed that Pollard and Walker were trying to stare down the mob. Then they stepped back into their warehouse and struggled to shut the door.

Up high, over the heads of the crowd, Mary Johnson's ax cut the air. Another ax caught the door and sliced it with a loud rip. The women backed away to avoid the spray of splinters. When the door gave way, they cheered as they charged into the store. Mary Jackson cringed. Their voices had an ominous ring.

She turned and saw more women running down the street. Small groups charged into stores along the way. Using axes, hammers, and broom handles, they bashed in doors and shattered windows. Women jostled with one another to get inside. In. Out. In. Out. People dragged sacks of sugar, flour, coffee, and tea.

Boots and shoes flew out of windows. The crowd scooped up the goods. Arms bulged with stolen clothing. Jewelry spilled out of pockets. In the midst of the mayhem, Mary heard a familiar, deep voice. "Anyone who is starving, follow me." It was William P. Munford, head of the Young Men's Christian Association. "We will feed you for free," he promised.

Some women stopped looting and followed Munford. But most refused. "We're not beggars." "We don't want charity." "We want fair prices," they shouted. A loud hiss ran through the crowd.

Richmond's Mayor Joseph Mayo climbed upon a nearby buggy and read from the Riot Act. "You are charged and commanded to immediately disperse and peaceably depart to your habitation or lawful business."

People rushed about as though he hadn't spoken, their clothing bloated with looted goods. Storekeepers slammed closed the shutters on their windows and tried to bolt their doors.

Mary fled up Fourteenth to Main, trying to get away from the uncontrollable mob. She could be stampeded. She pulled out her watch. It was ten o'clock. Would this morning ever end? And how would it turn out? She moved to the sidelines and watched a surge of women and men running by her. Someone threw a rock into the window of John C. Page's shoe store. Glass shattered and rained on the crowd. The crazed mob stormed inside.

She was in earshot when Governor Lechter arrived on a cart. "Any one of you suffering for want of bread or anything else has my sympathy and should be given relief as far as possible," he shouted. "However, I have no sympathy with mobs. As long as I am governor of Virginia, mobs will not be allowed, and I will use all my power to suppress them." He yelled to an aide to bring out the Public Guard. "You have five minutes to disperse before I give the order to shoot."

"Let the blind pigs come!" yelled a group of boys. "A pig without an eye is a blind pig." Richmond boys often ridiculed the Guard as pigs. On their hats the Public Guard wore the letters "P.G." Mary had forbidden her children from using these popular taunts.

She ran in anticipation of being fired upon. Hundreds were screaming as they ran up Franklin, to Twelfth Street. Please don't let me trip, Mary thought. Behind her, she heard the taunts about the Public Guard, then the clomping of horses. Was that Lieutenant Gay and the Public Guard? Someone shouted, "President Davis has come." She wanted to see him. He was a good family man. She respected that about him. Surely he could understand their need to feed their families.

But she had to get away from this crowd and the threat of getting fired upon. She pushed her way through the mob toward the Customs House.

She walked west in a daze. Past Sixth Street, the cross street of the Second Market. Then two blocks north to Broad Street. Then westward to First Street. She had to get home and away from the angry mob.

Someone gripped her arm tightly. "You're under arrest," the police officer said.

* * *

Court records and newspapers confirm that at least forty-four women and twenty-nine men were arrested. Most had their charges dropped or were acquitted. Mary Jackson was tried for a misdemeanor: inciting a riot and looting a store. There is no evidence whether or not she served any prison time. Mary Johnson was the only woman charged with a felony. She was found guilty of stealing bacon and sentenced to five years in the Virginia State Penitentiary. Four men were also charged.

The Confederate government tried to play down the bread riot. President Davis ordered the news quashed. Southern reporters wrote biased, exaggerated stories in the newspapers. Some wrote that the riot was caused by Northern sympathizers who had moved to

Richmond. According to eyewitnesses, about one thousand women were involved in the riot. The Richmond bread riot was the largest and most important of the many food riots in the South in the spring of 1863.

This event was not the last of looting in Richmond. Food shortages persisted, and so did theft.

Working-class people depended on the city for their water. When a flood from melting snow broke the city's pipes, people had to get water from an old well. The day after the bread riot, crowds gathered at this old well and were driven away by the City Battalion. Rumors circulated on April 10 about another riot. The Confederate War Department increased the number of soldiers in Richmond and stationed cannons downtown. The rumored riot never took place.

Although the City Council called the event on April 2 a "disgraceful riot," it did result in government action to get food to poor families. Overseers of the Poor were appointed and gave tickets to be used to purchase food at two markets in Richmond. But in the South, food remained scarce until the war ended.

"Flag All Free Without a Slave":
WILLIAM H. CARNEY

Massachusetts Governor John A. Andrew felt strongly that black men should fight in the war. After Lincoln's Emancipation Proclamation of January 1, 1863, he set out to create a model regiment of men of African descent. More than a thousand African American men from towns in Massachusetts and as far away as New York, Ohio, and Pennsylvania enlisted in Andrew's regiment. On May 28, 1863, Bostonians cheered the Massachusetts 54th Colored Infantry as it shipped out to help capture the important port city of Charleston, South Carolina.

The Confederacy controlled Fort Wagner on Morris Island, which protected the entrance to Charleston's harbor. Twenty-five-year-old Robert Gould Shaw, the white commander of the 54th, had volunteered his regiment to lead the attack on the fort.

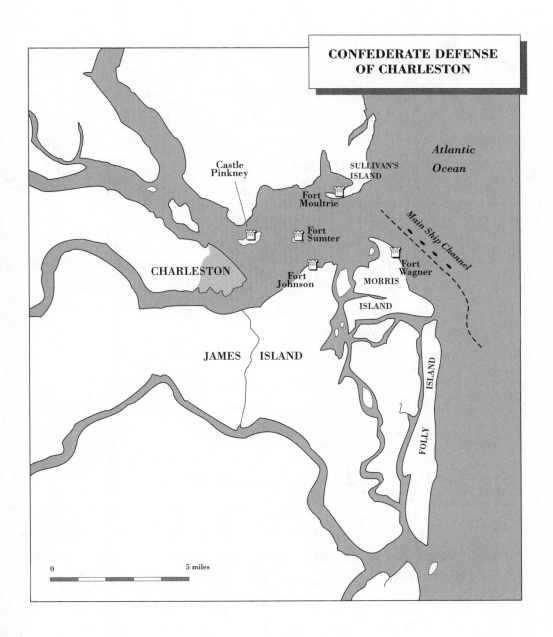

CONFEDERATE DEFENSE
OF CHARLESTON

Castle
Pinkney

SULLIVAN'S
ISLAND

Atlantic
Ocean

Fort
Moultrie

Main Ship Channel

Fort
Sumter

CHARLESTON

Fort
Wagner

Fort
Johnson

MORRIS

ISLAND

JAMES   ISLAND

FOLLY   ISLAND

0   5 miles

Twenty-three-year-old William H. Carney of Company C was exhausted and hot. So were the other men of the 54th Regiment. It was six-thirty in the evening. Confederate cannon fire exploded into the sand hills of Morris Island. Carney looked down the beach. In the early evening light, six hundred men in blue uniforms still stood in a tight column. It didn't appear that anyone from the regiment had been hit. No matter how fierce the fire, Carney knew, the 54th would hold the line.

"O, give us a flag all free without a slave . . ."

Someone began singing the regiment's marching song that a fellow soldier had written about free blacks fighting to save their country. Carney joined in. So did others around him. Their voices harmonized. The drummers sounded the beat.

> *"We'll fight to defend it as our fathers did so brave.*
> *We had a hard road to travel, but our day is coming*
>   *fast,*
> *For God is for the right, and we have no need to fear—*
> *The Union must be saved by the colored volunteer."*

Carney felt proud and determined. He had been born a slave in Norfolk, Virginia. His family moved north when his father earned his freedom. But as a child, he never thought that he would be fighting to emancipate his people. Now he was ready with his regiment to attack Fort Wagner. The Confederate big guns on Fort Sumter and the forts on James and Sullivan Islands were spewing fire into the marshes on the beach, making deep, wet craters. Clouds of smoke lingered over the salt water and blew about in the sea breezes. Still the 54th held its line. Carney knew the cannons would shoot directly at them once they charged the fort.

The low sun cast shadows on the beach. Carney tried to be patient, waiting for the order to charge. He knew it would come soon. His commander, Colonel Robert Gould Shaw, and General George Crockett Strong were eating supper in the general's tent, discussing the details of the attack.

Carney wished he had something to eat. The only thing anyone in his regiment had had today were scraps of soaked, stale bread.

More cannon blasts. His ears felt on fire. The regiment kept adjusting the line to avoid getting hit. He saw Sergeant John Wall roll up the Stars and Stripes. "Keep the flag safe from gunfire and capture" was a rule that every soldier knew. Carney straightened his back and stood tall in respect for the flag. He watched Corporal Peal holding his wooden staff high so that the state flag didn't touch the ground as he rolled the white silk on it with his free hand.

"Unfurl those colors!" ordered Captain William H. Simpkins from Company K.

The flag bearers immediately unrolled their silks. Carney enjoyed hearing the silk fabrics flutter in the sea breezes. Because of the breezes, not all the individual letters on the Stars and Stripes were visible, but he knew what it read. Across the center stripe were the words *54TH REGT US INFANTRY*, embroidered in silver. Yellow fringe hung from the flag's edges. Blue and white cords and tassels tied the flag to the almost-ten-foot-long staff.

Suddenly he heard the unexpected sound of horses' hooves beating the wet sand. Colonel Shaw was galloping toward them. Shaw was only two years older than Carney. He had enlisted in the army as soon as the South seceded, and had proved himself as captain with the Second Massachusetts last year at Front Royal, Cedar Mountain, and Antietam. When Governor John Andrew asked him to lead the 54th, Shaw had initially refused. He was white, and had feared a backlash among his peers if he led black soldiers. His mother, a staunch abolitionist, wrote him a letter asking him to change his mind. She made Shaw's more conservative father deliver it to their son in the field. Her letter worked. Carney was glad to have Shaw as his commander, and so were his comrades. He was a strict disciplinarian, but always fair. The regiment greatly respected him.

Tadadarum! Tadadarum! The two drummers from New Bedford, Massachusetts, where Carney lived, began to play. Rebel cannon shot drowned out the drumrolls. Thunder in the distance heightened the infernal blasting of the cannons. Storm clouds blew over the sea. High tide was coming in. Waves splashed against the legs of Shaw's horse.

How fine the colonel looked. His tight-fitting jacket had a silver eagle denoting his rank. The eagle shone brightly against the setting sun. His corded felt hat dipped and rose with his horse's gait.

His light blue trousers hugged his horse's flanks. His fancy English-made sword glistened.

Shaw dismounted close to Lieutenant-Colonel Hallowell, his second-in-command. "Break the column at the sixth company," instructed Shaw. "Lead your five companies to the rear of mine. We will advance east toward the beach."

Carney checked to make sure the bayonet was tight at the end of his rifle.

"Advance!" At Shaw's command, Carney and his fellow soldiers marched along the beach. The tide rushed against their ankles.

The fort was no more than fifteen hundred yards away.

"Halt," Shaw commanded. "Lie down."

Carney knew what to do: Rest and stay out of sight of the enemy gunners until support infantry arrived.

"Muskets loaded, but not capped. Bayonets fixed." Carney checked his weapon again.

He lay on his stomach in the moist sand, trying to ignore the vicious mosquitoes and sand flies biting him.

He saw fog rising from the sea. The sun dropped lower in the west. It would be dark soon. When would the support troops come? Waiting was so difficult.

A half hour later, he saw the first of the support troops march down the beach. Word spread up the ranks: It was the 6th Connecticut.

"Rise." Shaw's command rippled through the regiment. Carney

stood and shook off the cramps in his legs.

General Strong, with a yellow handkerchief around his neck, approached on a gray horse. At the head of the formation, Strong reined in his horse. "Boys, will you lead the column?"

"Yes!" the 54th roared.

"I am a Massachusetts man," Strong continued when the men quieted. "I know you will fight for the honor of the state." He lowered his voice and told them he was sorry they hadn't eaten or slept. He reminded them their enemy was also hungry and tired. Then he shouted his final, most important instruction. "Don't fire a musket on the way up." His horse reared. "Go in and bayonet them at their guns."

Strong looked to Sergeant Wall, the flag carrier. "If this man falls, who will carry the flag?" he asked.

"I will, sir." Shaw's voice was definitive. Carney felt proud of the colonel and proud to be following the Stars and Stripes into battle.

Strong saluted and then turned his horse back down the beach. Carney watched him disappear.

The sun set and it grew dark quickly. The mosquitoes were even more vicious now.

Carney felt tension all about him. His comrades were as anxious as he was for the attack to begin. Hallowell joined Shaw at the head of the troops.

"We shall take the fort or die there!" Shaw shouted.

The plan passed through the ranks: The two columns would

approach Fort Wagner in separate, sweeping lines, in wing formation. Shaw would lead the attack on the fort's heavily artilleried southern wall. Hallowell's men would approach the southeast wall. "I shall go in advance with the national flag," Shaw told Hallowell. "Keep the state flag with you. It will give the men something to rally round."

Shaw puffed on his cigar and walked up and down the line, inspecting his troops. Carney noticed the antique gem in his ring. Shaw checked the time on his gold pocket watch and looked at his soldiers. "I want you to prove yourselves. The eyes of thousands will be upon you."

Crash! Another Confederate cannonball exploded into the sand hills. The words of the chorus to their regiment's marching song soothed William Carney.

> *O, give us a flag all free without a slave,*
> *We'll fight to defend it as our fathers did so brave.*
> *We had a hard road to travel, but our day is coming*
> *   fast,*
> *For God is for the right, and we have no need to fear—*
> *The Union must be saved by the colored volunteer.*

The air was dark and thick. Carney smelled smoke. Down the line men were coughing. More cannonballs whirred overhead. They, too, missed their targets.

"Attention!" Shaw commanded. His sword glistened above their heads in the almost dark sky. "Move quick time to within a hundred yards of the fort. Then double quick, and charge."

Carney knew what Shaw was asking. Quick time meant 120 steps a minute; double quick, 165 steps. Strides must be thirty-three inches long. It would be hard to move that fast, but Carney would try, and so would the others, to do 165 a minute if need be.

"Use only the bayonet. Don't fire," Shaw ordered. "We'll have rifle support behind us." Then came the order Carney had been waiting for since the day he signed up.

"Forward!"

The column moved in wide, quick steps. This was the moment they had trained for. Darkness would not stop them. Carney kept his eyes on Colonel Shaw and the Union flag in Sergeant John Wall's able hands. The staff's eagle was raised high above the men's heads.

Step. Step. Suddenly the firing from Fort Wagner ceased. The quiet was frightening, for he knew the enemy could see them coming.

"Keep the alignment," ordered Shaw.

Blasts of cannon fire from the nearby forts opened up on them. But still they marched in wide, quick strides. "Tighten your ranks," the company officers shouted.

Quick step for a thousand yards down the beach. A bare sliver of light from the waning sun lit only the men in front of and next to Carney. The sound of cannon fire was everywhere. Thick smoke caught his breath. He tried to keep his eyes on the Stars and Stripes. Men to the extreme right of the column were waist-high in the water. They struggled to stay afoot. The sand grew even narrower. Carney and those to his left were squeezed together into the wet marsh. Only the men in the middle stood on a dry patch of sand in between the water and the marsh.

Keep the pace. Quick time!

The fort loomed less than two hundred yards ahead. Quartz sand and turf-covered palmetto logs formed the fort's embankments. Higher sand protected its tall southern wall. The huge structure blazed before Carney's eyes as rebel rifle and cannon fire exploded around him. His comrades fell into the craters created by the blasts. The flashes of rifle fire momentarily blinded Carney. Then he made out arms and heads of Confederate soldiers shooting down at him. He stumbled on the uneven ground. Bodies and clumps of sand and debris lay in his path. He tried not to look at the dead sprawled everywhere.

If only he could cross the wide, wet trench separating them from the southern wall, a mere one hundred yards away. Pick up the pace. Widen the stride. He trudged through three feet of water in the trench. He fought to keep his balance. His tired calf muscles stretched with every step. He felt as if he was being swallowed up. Rifle fire exploded all about him. His boots were heavy with water soaked with other soldiers' blood. But he kept moving. Suddenly Carney clutched his thigh. He had been shot. He had to keep moving. He dragged his wounded leg.

He saw John Wall fall into the trench. Colonel Shaw grabbed the staff and colors.

"Double quick!" Shaw commanded. "Forward, Fifty-fourth! We will not be defeated."

Faster. Faster. He was half crawling now.

The rebels on the parapet fired at short range.

Carney lifted his bayonet high and charged. So did his comrades. Forward, forward. A blaze of fire greeted them. Still they charged.

Now Shaw was on the parapet waving the Stars and Stripes and his sword. Bleeding, he fell backward down the slope from the parapet. Carney saw the flag trailing to the ground. He plunged into the steady fire and caught the staff. He stood it on the parapet, then squatted below the wall of the fort for cover. Where was the state flag? He looked about and saw it was also planted on the fort.

We will not be defeated!

Confederate soldiers tore at the flag, but Carney held tight. He would die before he would let them take it. He watched helplessly as they wrested the state silk free from Henry Peal, but they could not steal the staff away from Peal.

Two more shots pierced Carney's body. He felt dizzy and light-headed. His fingers were numb. Hold on, hold on. He clutched the Union flagstaff.

Confederate grenades lit the area as brightly as day even though

it was midnight. Where were the reinforcements?

"Form in line," shouted Captain Luis Emilio. "Retreat!" Emilio was only nineteen years old. He was youngest of all the regiment's nine officers. If he was giving orders, that meant the other officers were dead or wounded.

Carney's ears ached from the noise. It was hard to focus now. He knew he had lost a lot of blood. He wasn't sure he could stand. But he would bring the flag back, no matter what. He tried to stand, but couldn't. The weight of the staff tripped him. He stumbled. He was too weak to walk. He moved forward on his knees, holding the flag above the ground. One knee, the next knee, he made his way.

At the field hospital, safe from the gunfire, Carney handed over the colors and fell. He heard the cheers of his fellow soldiers. "Boys, I only did my duty," he said modestly. "The old flag never touched the ground."

* * *

The support troops did not move fast enough to help the 54th regiment. If they had, the Union might have captured Fort Wagner. Tragically, when support came, in the darkness some white soldiers fired at the backs of the 54th. Black soldiers felt that they were betrayed by the white troops in their delay. Some historians have agreed.

The Union loss at Fort Wagner was 1,515 killed or wounded, including 111 officers. One hundred eighteen of the 1,700 Confederate soldiers were killed or wounded.

Only 600 of the 1,000 soldiers in the 54th fought at Fort Wagner. Some were on St. Helena Island as guards; some were wounded before the attack. Many were digging defensive ditches elsewhere. Of the 600, 212 men were killed or wounded. Sixty men were captured. Colonel Shaw and General Strong were fatally wounded.

The attack on Fort Wagner proved to white Americans that black Americans were courageous and willing to fight for the Union. General Ulysses S. Grant called the black soldier *"a powerful ally."* President Lincoln praised the regiment. When the Union captured Charleston in February 1865, the soldiers of the Massachusetts 54th Regiment were among the first federal troops to enter the city.

About 180,000 African Americans fought in the Civil War. Black Americans made up only one percent of the population of the North, but they made up twelve percent of Union forces.

Confederate hostility toward black soldiers extended to their white commander. Rebel soldiers showed their contempt for Shaw by placing his body in a mass grave with the bodies of his men. Shaw's father decided it was an honor for his son to lie with his troops and requested that his remains be left there. In October 1864 the Massachusetts 54th Regiment and former Sea Island (South Carolina) slaves founded the Shaw School for the black children of Charleston. They collected $2,832 in his honor.

Carney was honorably discharged in 1864 because of his wounds. He returned to New Bedford, Massachusetts, and worked for thirty-two years as a mail carrier. He married one of the first black female *teachers in the state. Records do not indicate that they had children. Carney frequently spoke to schoolchildren about how he saved the flag.*

Carney received the Congressional Medal of Honor in 1900. When he died in 1908, the state flag was lowered to half-mast.

"Full Speed Ahead!":
DAVID GLASGOW FARRAGUT

For two years Union ships had blockaded many Southern ports to keep goods from coming in and going out. Cotton exports to England had dropped from 816 million pounds a year to 200 million pounds. But Confederate blockade-runners could still enter the South through Mobile Bay on the Gulf of Mexico. The city of Mobile, Alabama, was a manufacturing center and an important railroad terminal. Union control of Mobile Bay would paralyze Southern trade and prevent Confederate troops and supplies from going north by train or ship.

In December 1863 President Abraham Lincoln asked sixty-three-year-old naval commander David Glasgow Farragut to prepare to attack Mobile. But capturing the city would be difficult. Its shallow water entrance was protected by three forts, a massive ironclad, and a minefield of torpedoes. On August 4, 1864, Farragut readied his men for attack.

It was almost sundown. The hot, humid August air had given way to fierce rain and more mosquitoes than usual. But at last the first part of Commander David Glasgow Farragut's plan of attack was under way. The gunboats were firing at Fort Gaines to distract the five hundred Confederate soldiers inside. Gaines was only one of the three forts protecting the entrance into the city.

Fort Morgan was the real problem. To get into the bay, Farragut had to guide his ships out of range of Morgan's cannons. His fleet had to pass through a minefield of torpedoes hidden under the water at the bay's entrance. These tin cones, filled two-thirds of the way with gunpowder, could destroy a ship on contact.

Farragut breathed in the familiar smell of salt and sea. He looked about the deck of his flagship, the USS *Hartford.* She had been his ship since her maiden voyage at the end of 1861. He had stood upon her deck when the Union captured New Orleans two years ago. Now he was commanding her in battle again.

He retired to his cabin for some quiet and wrote what he believed could be his last letter to his wife.

> *My dearest Wife,*
> *I write and leave this letter for you. I am going into Mobile Bay in the morning if "God is my leader" as I hope He is, and in Him I place my trust; if He thinks it is the proper place for me to die, I am ready to submit to His will. . . . God bless and preserve you, my darling,*

and my dear Boy, if anything should happen to me and may His blessings also rest upon your dear Mother and all your sisters and their children. Your devoted and affectionate husband, who never for one moment forgot his love, duty, or fidelity to you, his devoted and best of wives.

Sleep did not come easily that night. The naval battle would begin tomorrow before dawn. He knew the fighting would be fierce and that many of his men would die. He himself might not survive.

At three o'clock in the morning, he answered a knock on the cabin door. His second-in-command, Captain Percival Drayton, brought good news. A southwest breeze was blowing into the bay. If it lasted, smoke from the battle would blow directly into the eyes of the Confederate gunners and block their vision.

He called his men together to review the plan for the last time. The fleet would enter at flood tide when the water was high. Attached to each ironclad would be a steam-powered gunboat.

No one spoke of it, but Farragut knew his men wondered, Is it possible to get through the bay? He wondered himself. There was only a quarter-mile-wide channel with no explosives and water high enough for ships to pass through. And this narrow channel was within range of Fort Morgan's cannons and the big guns of the Confederate ironclad *Tennessee*.

The *Hartford* will go first, Farragut announced.

The *Brooklyn* should be first, his officers countered. She had a torpedo-sweeping device. The *Hartford* had none.

Farragut resisted their suggestion. He believed it was a commander's duty to lead his fleet into battle. The *Brooklyn* is so much stronger, they argued. She had four chase bow guns compared to the *Hartford*'s two.

Reluctantly Farragut agreed to have his ship go second.

No firing, he instructed, until they were as close as possible to the fort. But *if* they were fired on, they were to fire back. He addressed the final issue: "Take care to pass near the easternmost buoy, which is clear of torpedoes."

Two and a half hours later the fleet was in proper formation. A hot breeze was still blowing into the bay. Farragut heard the silks of the Stars and Stripes on each vessel flap in the breeze as his fleet moved slowly into the bay. It was five-thirty in the morning and still dark. How long until the Confederates saw them and fired?

At daylight, an hour later, he heard Fort Morgan's cannons roaring at the *Brooklyn*. The ship's gunners fired back. Suddenly Farragut was thrown off balance. His ship had been hit. More blasts and shouts. His men scrambled for cover. The wounded were sprawled on the deck. Blood and thick black smoke were everywhere. Farragut gasped for air.

More deafening cannon fire. What about the rest of his fleet? He could not see the other ships from deck level. He needed to get

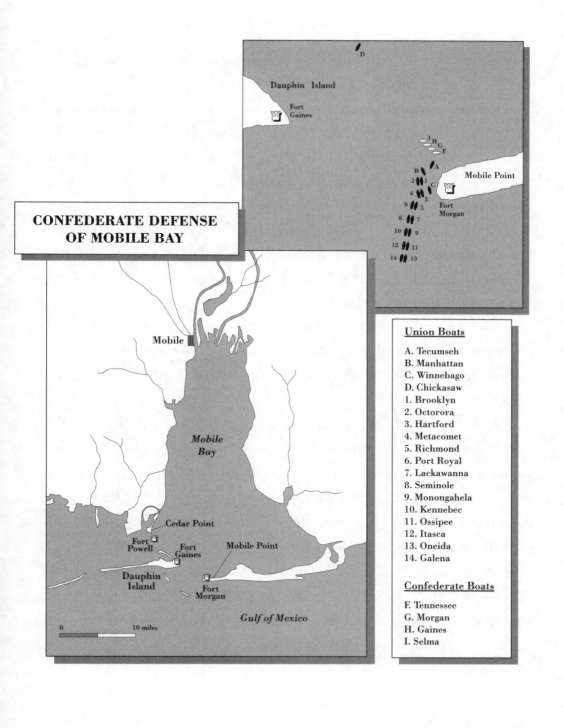

CONFEDERATE DEFENSE OF MOBILE BAY

Dauphin Island

Fort Gaines

Mobile Point

Fort Morgan

Mobile

Mobile Bay

Cedar Point

Fort Powell

Fort Gaines

Mobile Point

Dauphin Island

Fort Morgan

Gulf of Mexico

0   10 miles

Union Boats

A. Tecumseh
B. Manhattan
C. Winnebago
D. Chickasaw
1. Brooklyn
2. Octorora
3. Hartford
4. Metacomet
5. Richmond
6. Port Royal
7. Lackawanna
8. Seminole
9. Monongahela
10. Kennebec
11. Ossipee
12. Itasca
13. Oneida
14. Galena

Confederate Boats

F. Tennessee
G. Morgan
H. Gaines
I. Selma

above the smoke. There was only one thing to do: Climb the rigging. Up he went. Twenty feet. Thirty feet. Forty feet.

Drayton saw him begin his ascent, but within seconds, Farragut was out of view. Had he been thrown overboard? Flung to the deck? If Farragut had reached the rigging, he had to be protected from falling. There was only one way to do that: Tie him to the rigging. Could it be done? Drayton ordered his signal quartermaster to try.

Up he climbed. Twenty feet. Thirty feet. Forty feet. When Quartermaster Knowles was level with Farragut, Knowles fastened a piece of lead line to one of the iron rods connecting the topmast rigging with the lower rigging.

"Never mind," Farragut shouted. "I'm all right."

Knowles ignored Farragut's order and tied the line around him.

Crash! Fort Morgan's cannons exploded with their deadly assault.

Farragut raised his spyglass to look at his fleet. Sailors on the Union *Lackawanna* were running away from their posts to dodge Confederate fire. He understood why: Many of these young men had never been in battle before and were terrified. Suddenly he saw the men run back to their posts. He had trained his officers well. As ever, they were alert and forceful.

He looked toward the *Chickasaw.* Standing on top of one turret was the captain. Confederate fire was all about him, but still he stood, waving his cap and shouting orders. Twenty-seven-year-old Captain Perkins was a brave young man.

The constant cannon blasts were ear-piercing. The smoke grew even thicker. An hour passed. Farragut was still on the rigging when he saw the massive Confederate *Tennessee* and three Confederate gunboats move toward his fleet.

The *Tennessee* was the mightiest ironclad in the Confederate navy. It was more powerful than any Union ironclad. Built to ram and sink ships, she had iron armor on all sides. Some of her cannons were in permanent positions. Others, on rotating platforms, fired in any direction. On her bow was a torpedo fixture.

Franklin Buchanan commanded the mighty *Tennessee*. Like Farragut, Buchanan was a Southerner. The two men had served together in the Union navy before the war. Farragut had disagreed with "Buck's" decision to go with the Confederacy, but he respected him as an adversary.

Suddenly Farragut saw one of his ironclads, the *Tecumseh,* turn off course. Why was she turning? Where was she going? Farragut watched her creep forward until she blocked the *Brooklyn* and the other ships behind. What was going on? The *Tecumseh* was on the wrong side of the buoy!

Boom! Farragut watched, stunned, as the *Tecumseh* careened to one side. A torpedo had exploded under the ship. The *Tecumseh's* stern lifted high in the air. Her propeller turned as she pitched out of sight. Immense steam bubbles soared above the water's surface. Farragut couldn't believe how fast she was sinking. It took thirty seconds at the most. Would any of the 114 men aboard escape?

Then silence in the bay. The Confederate cannons had stopped firing. Farragut knew that Buchanan had seen the disaster and was giving him time to rescue his men.

Farragut shouted through the voice tube to send a boat out to rescue the survivors.

O God, who created man and gave him reason, direct me what to do. Shall I go on? he prayed silently.

If he won this battle, he could close the seaport of Mobile. It would help cripple the South, and perhaps end the war sooner rather than later. He knew there were more torpedoes ahead. But these explosives had been in the water for at least six weeks. Not all of them would be functioning now. To succeed, he had only one choice: Go full speed ahead. Yes, it was the duty of an officer to save as many of his men as possible, but in battle there was always sacrifice and death. He was not asking his men to do anything that he himself would not do.

"I'll lead." Farragut shouted through the voice tube to the pilot to take a northwest course.

The cannons of Fort Morgan roared again. They spewed more fire and noise as the *Hartford* moved to the front of the fleet. As she passed the *Brooklyn*, her captain, James Alden, informed Farragut that he saw a heavy line of torpedoes across the narrow entry channel. It was a risk that had to be taken. Cannon fire blasted the *Hartford* as she moved on toward the minefield area.

Now she was right in the center of the explosives. The next

second would determine if he were right or wrong. He held his breath and listened. Silence. The torpedoes were dead. His gamble had paid off.

Now his fleet was inside the bay, beyond the range of Fort Morgan's guns, but not beyond danger from the *Tennessee*. The Confederate ironclad headed toward his ship. But the *Hartford* was faster, and the *Tennessee* couldn't get up enough speed to ram back. The two vessels passed alongside each other, their cannons firing away. Farragut smelled smoke and blood everywhere. He shuddered, thinking about how many men on both sides would die in this battle.

He saw the *Tennessee* withdraw from the battle. Buchanan must have realized he could not win at this time. But Farragut knew Buck would not surrender. He would continue fighting, but not now. Farragut watched triumphantly as the Confederate *Gaines*, crippled by gunfire, was run up onto the beach behind Fort Morgan. The Union *Metacomet* sank the *Selma*. The Confederate *Morgan* managed to flee to safety.

At eight thirty-five A.M., Farragut's fleet regrouped. There were boisterous cheers and hurrahs. The first part of the battle was over, and they were in the bay. But they still had to capture the *Tennessee*. Farragut would let his men rest until dark. Tonight he would order his fleet to go after the *Tennessee*.

But twenty-five minutes later, Farragut saw the *Tennessee* heading straight toward his ships. Ever determined, Buck might not win this battle, but Farragut knew he was going to try to inflict as much damage as possible on Farragut's fleet.

Farragut ordered the signal sent to all ships: Run down the *Tennessee.*

One by one the Union ironclads rammed the *Tennessee.* They hardly injured her; yet they were badly battered. But that did not stop his officers. Again and again they ordered their ships to ram the *Tennessee.*

Finally, success. The *Tennessee*'s gun port was hit. One cannon could no longer fire. Still the mighty *Tennessee* plowed on. It was coming straight toward the *Hartford.* Farragut knew it was now a battle between him and Buck. He ordered the *Hartford* turned around in order to ram the *Tennessee.* More speed, he commanded. The Confederate *Tennessee* was moving more slowly than before. Farragut saw that her smokestack had been hit. Her steam engine was damaged.

The two ironclads moved closer still. It looked as if they were going to collide. At the last second, Buchanan turned the *Tennessee* slightly. Now the vessels were alongside each other. Their guns were so close they almost touched as they blasted away. The noise was deafening. Sailors on both sides screamed as they were hit.

Then only one blast sounded from the *Tennessee.* Most of her cannons had been hit and could not fire. Farragut's fleet continued firing away at the wounded ship.

The mighty Confederate ram tilted into the water. Union gunfire had penetrated her casement.

Farragut could not see that Buchanan was hit and wedged under a piece of metal. He did not hear Buchanan order his second-in-command to take over. All Farragut could see was the Confederate battle flag being lowered and a white flag raised. The battle for Mobile Bay was won.

* * *

Ninety-three men went down on the Union ship the Tecumseh; *only twenty-one escaped. Fifty-two other Northern naval men died. One hundred seventy were wounded. On the Confederate side, Buchanan and eleven others were killed and twenty wounded. That night Farragut wrote his wife:*

> *The Almighty has smiled upon me once more. I am in Mobile Bay. . . . It was a hard fight. . . . Sad to say, the* Tecumseh *was sunk by a torpedo, and poor Craven with his gallant crew went to the bottom. I have lost a number of fine fellows, more than ever before. . . . [The Confederates] made a gallant fight, but was all to no purpose. . . . I escaped, thank God! without a scratch. God bless you, and make you as thankful for this victory as I am.*

Many history books state that Farragut yelled, "Damn the torpedoes, full speed ahead!" when he ordered his pilot to go into the minefield

IOWA

Chicago

ILLINOIS

INDIANA

OHIO

PENNSYLVANIA

KANSAS
TERRITORY

MISSOURI

Great Northern Railroad

St. Louis

Cincinnati

WEST
VIRGINIA

VIRGINIA

Mobile and Ohio Railroad

KENTUCKY

INDIAN
TERRITORY

ARKANSAS

TENNESSEE

NORTH CAROLINA

SOUTH
CAROLINA

TEXAS

LOUISIANA

MISSISSIPPI

ALABAMA

GEORGIA

Mobile Bay

Mobile

*Atlantic
Ocean*

Fort
Gaines

Fort
Morgan

FLORIDA

Gulf of Mexico

STRATEGIC LOCATION
OF MOBILE BAY

0   200 miles

of torpedoes. There are no primary sources from that time to confirm what he said or did not say at that moment. The statement "Damn the torpedoes, full speed ahead!" came into the mythology of the Civil War twenty years after the fact.

Sixty-three-year-old David Glasgow Farragut was born in Tennessee, raised in Louisiana, and lived in Virginia. His roots in the Union began with his father, Jorge Anthony Magin Farragut, who emigrated from Minorca, an island off the east coast of Spain, in 1776. Inspired by the American Revolution, Jorge fought with the colonists. He continued his naval service in the War of 1812.

Captain Craven of the Tecumseh *turned his ship because he saw the* Tennessee *moving toward the Union fleet. He wanted to block her by putting his ship between her and the other Union ships to protect them from Buchanan's fleet.*

Franklin Buchanan was born in Maryland, a border state with slaves. When the war broke out, he felt certain that his home state would side with the Confederacy. He resigned from the Union navy. When Maryland did not leave the Union, he tried to withdraw his resignation. But Navy Secretary Gideon Welles would not allow it, so Buchanan joined the Confederate navy.

"With Malice Toward None":

ABRAHAM LINCOLN
and
NOAH BROOKS

On Friday, March 4, 1865, Abraham Lincoln was inaugurated for his second term as president. Tens of thousands of Americans came by train from as far away as California to attend the inauguration. Under the leadership of General Ulysses S. Grant, Union troops were laying siege to Petersburg, Virginia, only twenty miles south of Richmond. That, combined with recent victories in Savannah, Georgia; Columbia and Charleston, South Carolina; and Wilmington, North Carolina, made Northerners feel hopeful about winning the four-year war.

Thirty-five-year-old Noah Brooks had been the Washington correspondent for the Sacramento Daily Union for three years. He had met Lincoln in 1855 in Dixon, Illinois, and admired him immediately for his eloquence and directness. Despite the twenty years' difference in their ages, the two men were friends. Brooks had stood near Lincoln when he announced the Emancipation Proclamation

*from the White House window. He visited the Lincoln family almost
every day. But Noah Brooks had no advance knowledge of Lincoln's
actual speech. Like many Northerners, he hoped Lincoln would speak
about how to reunify the country once this bitter war was over.*

* * *

Noah Brooks took a seat in the press gallery of the U.S. Senate and
checked his pocket watch. Only 10:30 A.M. The official ceremony
would not begin for another half hour. What a day for an inauguration! The morning had brought pounding rain. There were at least
ten inches of mud on the streets. That hadn't stopped people from
coming out or dressing up. But it was a sad sight seeing all those
women with their hoop skirts splashed and streaked with mud.
There were also soldiers everywhere. They were on the roads leading to the city, on horseback at major intersections, and on rooftops
with rifles. Plainclothes detectives were out looking for suspicious
people. He had heard rumors that Lincoln might be kidnapped or
assassinated.

Despite the rain, spirits were high at the inaugural parade. Each
group tried to outdo the next. The competition was great among the
nation's fire companies. Philadelphia's firefighters stood out with
their red shirts blazing against black coats and pants. The crowd
applauded most for the capital's fire company with its horse-drawn
steam engines. But the loudest cheers were for the Forty-fifth
Regiment U.S. Colored Troops and African-American Odd Fellows.

It was the first time black soldiers had marched in an inaugural procession. Of course there was cheering and shouting when the presidential coach passed, but only Mrs. Lincoln was in it. Where was the president?

The chatter of people filing into the Senate distracted Brooks. Retiring vice president Hannibal Hamlin was entering arm in arm with the new vice president, Andrew Johnson. Was Johnson leaning on Hamlin? It looked that way.

Every notable in government seemed to be there. Brooks recognized almost all the members of Congress. Attorney General James Speed, Secretary of War Edwin M. Stanton, and Secretary of the Navy Gideon Welles came in together. Rear Admiral David G. Farragut and Brigadier General Joseph Hooker followed, resplendent in full military dress. Where was Frederick Douglass? He had to be somewhere. And where were the Lincolns? Why weren't they here yet?

The seats filled quickly, and the crowded chamber warmed up. Brooks's face became moist from heat and dampness.

Vice President Hamlin walked toward the podium, and the buzz settled down. Hamlin had not spoken more than a few words when Secretary of State William Seward and the nine Supreme Court justices entered the chamber. Hamlin realized he had lost his audience and stopped speaking until they were seated. The elderly justices look very dignified in their black robes, Brooks thought.

Hamlin began again. And again, he was interrupted, this time by

Mrs. Lincoln entering the diplomatic gallery. Where was the president?

Mrs. Lincoln took her seat, and the vice president picked up where he left off, thanking Congress for its many kindnesses. "I wish my friend and worthy successor no higher success than the same relations between him and yourselves." Hamlin's speech was short and to the point, Brooks thought.

Hamlin introduced his successor. Andrew Johnson had been a Democratic senator from Tennessee when the war broke out. He tried to prevent his state from seceding, but Tennessee voted overwhelmingly to join the Confederacy. Johnson was the only Southern senator who remained loyal to the North. The Republicans had rewarded him with the vice presidential nomination.

Johnson turned his head and nodded, as if acknowledging everyone in the room. Was it his imagination? Was Johnson a little unsteady on his feet? Brooks wondered. Lincoln entered the chamber, and Brooks was distracted from Johnson's opening sentences. No matter, really. He didn't expect to take many notes. Johnson's speech would be short. Vice presidents always gave short speeches.

Lincoln sat down. Brooks returned his attention to Johnson. The vice president was slurring his words. With each new sentence, the slurring got worse and his thoughts more meandering. Brooks didn't want to believe it, but there was no doubt about it. The vice president was drunk.

Brooks saw Attorney General James Speed whisper to Secretary of War Edwin Stanton. Stanton's face stiffened. He whispered to the secretary of the navy, Gideon Welles. Would they try to stop Johnson's speech? What must the president be feeling, listening to such drivel? This drunken man was his vice president. Brooks looked at Lincoln's hunched shoulders and his bowed head.

The speech dragged on. After ten minutes Hamlin pulled on Johnson's coattails, hoping to get his attention. He didn't. Finally, after another five minutes, Johnson stopped speaking and was sworn in.

He called the Senate to order. But he was too drunk to read out the names of the newly elected senators, so John W. Forney, secretary of the Senate, took over. Brooks saw Lincoln lean to talk to one of the marshals. If only he could hear what Lincoln said. He felt certain it had to do with Johnson.

At 11:45 A.M. the ceremonies moved outside. The sky was still gray, but there were no clouds. Brooks looked out on a sea of white and black faces. The military brass bands blared until Senate Sergeant-at-Arms George T. Brown bowed, his shiny black top hat in hand. Almost immediately the crowd quieted. "Ladies and gentlemen, the president of the United States," he said.

A swell of cheers and hurrahs. Drums boomed, and the brass blared. The bands played "Hail to the Chief." The applause finally subsided, but the cheering continued for a full five minutes.

Abraham Lincoln stood before a small white iron table and looked out over the crowd. Brooks still marveled at Lincoln's height. At six foot four inches, he dwarfed most men. He was fifty-six years

old, but his long, lanky frame was like a young man's, though his body was ungraceful. It had always been ungraceful. He was square shouldered. His long arms hung awkwardly by his side. Ten years ago when Brooks had first met Lincoln, he was struck by his erect posture. Now Lincoln stooped. Carrying the nation's burdens the past four years had also dulled his eyes and lined his face beyond his years. Some people found his face ugly and common. They mocked his large ears. Lincoln cared little about what he wore or how he looked. His hair usually appeared uncombed, even when it was combed, as it was today. But Brooks found Lincoln's face open and honest; he was a plain man, a man of the people.

Lincoln held the speech in his left hand. He adjusted his steel-rimmed glasses with his right hand. "Fellow-Countrymen," he began. The crowd applauded once more.

"Bless the Lord, bless the Lord," shouted a group of black spectators.

Suddenly the wind stopped blowing, and the sun, hidden all day, flooded the area with light. Brooks's heart beat quicker. Please let this unexpected clearing be a hopeful sign that the darkness of the past four years is passing, he prayed.

The president continued: ". . . Four years ago all thoughts were anxiously directed to an impending civil war. All dreaded it, all sought to avert it. While the inaugural address was being delivered from this place, devoted altogether to saving the Union without war, insurgent agents were in the city seeking to destroy it without war—

seeking to dissolve the Union and divide effects by negotiation. Both parties deprecated war, but one of them would make war rather than let the nation survive, and the other would accept war rather than let it perish. . . ."

Brooks cheered and applauded along with everyone. Lincoln waited for the roar of approval to die down. Then he said, "And the war came."

Yes, it was true, Brooks thought. All Americans—Southerners and Northerners—had dreaded the idea of war. But the North could not let the South secede. When the South attacked Fort Sumter, there was no choice for the North but to take up arms and fight to preserve the Union.

Lincoln continued: "One-eighth of the whole population were colored slaves. . . . These slaves constituted a peculiar and powerful interest. All knew that this interest was somehow the cause of the war."

"Bless the Lord, bless the Lord." Black spectators punctuated almost every sentence.

"To strengthen, perpetuate, and extend this interest was the object for which the insurgents would rend the Union even by war. . . ."

Again, the truth, thought Noah Brooks. Everyone knew Lincoln's original intention had been to restrict slavery to the South, not to confront and dismantle it. He had changed his mind.

"Neither party expected for the war the magnitude or the duration which it has already attained. . . ." Lincoln slowed his rhythm and spoke more distinctly. "Both read the same Bible and pray to the same God, and each invokes His aid against the other. It may seem strange that any men should dare to ask a just God's assistance in wringing their bread from the sweat of other men's faces, but let us judge not, that we be not judged."

Except for the constant interjections of "Bless the Lord," the crowd was silent.

Perhaps they are digesting his last phrase, Brooks thought. "Let us judge not, that we be not judged" was a variation of a verse from Isaiah in the Old Testament.

Noah recognized from Lincoln's solemn tone that the president was close to concluding his thoughts: "The prayers of both could not be answered. That of neither has been answered fully. The Almighty has His own purposes. . . . Fondly do we hope, fervently do we pray, that this mighty scourge of war may speedily pass away."

Brooks bowed his head. Victory *had* to come to the North. He could not bear to think what would happen to the country if it did not. But when the North triumphed, what would be next? How would the country ever heal its wounds from this bitter struggle? What could Lincoln do to repair the Union? He listened as Lincoln answered his unspoken question.

"With malice toward none, with charity for all, with firmness in the right as God gives us to see the right, let us strive on to finish the work we are in, to bind up the nation's wounds, to care for him who shall have borne the battle and for his widow and his orphan, to do all which may achieve and cherish a just and lasting peace among ourselves and with all nations."

The speech was over. Brooks blinked away tears. He was a reporter, trained to be objective, but Lincoln's eloquence deeply moved him. The president was a noble man with noble words. He always found the right phrase for the occasion. He had spoken the truth today. If the country was to move forward, the North and South had to reconcile. There could be no revenge. The North had to reach out and help the South. The South was in shambles. Its buildings, homes, factories, and farms were burned to the ground. Its rich fields that brought forth cotton were abandoned.

He knew what the president meant when he used the word *charity*. He did not mean giving money to those in need. He meant charity as in loving others, loving even thy enemies, as written in the New Testament. And in time, the enemy would become a friend again. This was the work ahead for the nation. War was not the end; it was the beginning of a new life for the country.

Lincoln placed his left hand on the open Bible and raised his right hand. He repeated after Chief Justice Chase the words of the presidential oath: "I do solemnly swear that I will faithfully execute the office of president of the United States, and will to the best of my ability, preserve, protect, and defend the Constitution of the United States." He paused. "So help me God," he concluded the oath. Then he kissed the Bible.

Now the applause was volcanic. The cheering and hurrahs were louder than Brooks had ever heard as a reporter. Military cannons overpowered the brass bands accompanying the cheers. Lincoln bowed.

Noah Brooks looked at his watch. 12:17 P.M. March 4, 1865. Abraham Lincoln was beginning his second term as president.

* * *

In the Sacramento Daily Union, *Noah Brooks praised President Lincoln's Second Inaugural Address and described Andrew Johnson's drunkenness. Brooks found out later that Lincoln was late for the inauguration because he was signing bills in the Capitol. He never wrote in his article the reason why Johnson was drunk. Perhaps he never found out that Johnson had taken whiskey that morning because he believed it would help him recover from typhoid fever. But the whiskey went to his head and caused the drunkenness.*

The full text of Lincoln's address was printed in newspapers all over the United States. The New York Herald *found the speech disappointing because Lincoln did not speak about foreign affairs. The* New York World *criticized Lincoln's inability to help the divided nation with "words of wisdom" and "words of hope." The* Chicago Times *said: "Lincoln's ideas and sentiments were childish." Yet the* Washington Daily National Intelligencer *praised the final paragraph as deserving "to be printed in gold." The* Jersey City Times *thought it "grand in its simplicity." Editorials in the few Southern papers that covered the speech were not favorable. Abolitionist leader Frederick Douglass greatly admired the speech, which he said was "more like a sermon than a state paper."*

Soon after the speech, the words "With malice toward none, with charity for all" were seen on souvenir badges, medals, and ribbons. Today people from all over the world can read this address on the north wall of the Lincoln Memorial in the nation's capital.

The Surrender:

ULYSSES S. GRANT
and
ROBERT E. LEE

On April 3, 1865, the Confederate capital of Richmond fell to the Union. Commander of all Confederate forces Robert E. Lee led his 30,000 troops to meet up with General Joseph E. Johnston. Johnston commanded the only Confederate Army in the East. Their plan was that, once united, the two armies would begin fighting again. Ulysses S. Grant, General-in-Chief of the U.S. Army, set out to block Lee from reaching Johnston. As Lee's army marched, Grant's troops attacked from many different directions.

More than 620,000 men—Northerners and Southerners—had been killed in battle over the past four years. Like President Lincoln, Grant wanted to end the war as soon as possible and avoid further bloodshed. On April 7, 1865, Grant sent Lee a letter asking him to surrender. Grant believed that if Lee would surrender his army, the rest of the Confederate forces would also surrender, for Lee was the supreme commander of all Confederate forces.

It was dark when the courier from Ulysses S. Grant caught up with General Robert E. Lee and his troops marching toward the village of Appomattox Court House, Virginia. Lee hoped to find much-needed food and supplies there. He read Grant's note carefully:

> *The results of the last week must convince you of the hopelessness of further resistance. I regard it as my duty to shift from myself the responsibility of any further blood, by asking of you the surrender of that portion of the C.S.A. [Confederate States Army] known as the Army of Northern Virginia.*

Lee gave the note to his lieutenant general. "Not yet," James Longstreet said, handing it back.

Lee was torn. Since January he had known that the North was closing in on the South. He appreciated Longstreet's faith in the Southern cause, but his men were exhausted. They had not eaten in five days. Every day more soldiers deserted. Many were too tired to walk. They fell out of line to lie down on the muddy ground, and many did not have the strength to get up. The horses and mules were tired and hungry too. Lee wrote back to Grant without showing his response to any of his officers.

I have received your note. Though not entertaining the hopelessness of further resistance on the part of my army, I reciprocate your desire to avoid useless effusion of blood. Before considering your proposition, I ask the terms you will offer on condition of its surrender.

Over the next two days, Grant and Lee exchanged two more notes. Lee finally agreed to meet. He felt uncertain about what the outcome of the meeting would be, but if it was to be surrender, he wanted to arrange the details himself. His father had told him how British commander Lord Cornwallis sent a stand-in to the surrender ceremony at the end of the Revolutionary War. Lee grew up believing that this act had diminished Cornwallis's brilliant career. He would not shirk this responsibility. He owed it to his men. He owed it to Virginia. He owed it to the Confederacy. He instructed his military secretary, Lieutenant Colonel Charles Marshall, to find a place for the meeting. He reminded Marshall to get permission from the owner.

Fifty-eight-year-old Lee got ready for the meeting. His silver-gray hair and full beard were neatly trimmed. His gray uniform was immaculately clean and pressed. He buttoned his jacket to his throat. His handsome boots, like his uniform, were barely travel stained. He donned his long sword. Its hilt was studded with many colored jewels. A gray felt hat that matched his uniform and a pair of long buckskin gloves completed his outfit. He called for his orderly to bring his horse, Traveller.

Ulysses S. Grant had a migraine headache that had lasted for three days. He had bathed his feet in hot water and mustard. He had stuck mustard plasters to his wrists and the back of his neck. Nothing stopped the pounding in his head. On top of constant pain, he was exhausted. He hadn't slept all night. The last thing he wanted to do today was ride across the Virginia countryside with the hope of boxing in Lee's troops. But he had no choice. He tugged on his horse's reins, signaling his officers to ready the men to march. Lieutenant Colonel Theodore S. Bowers, Brigadier General John Rawlins, and Lieutenant Colonel Ely S. Parker took the lead.

A mile later a soldier galloped down the muddy clay road toward them. Was it another note from Lee? Grant read this one silently. Then, without showing any emotion in his voice or on his face, he asked John Rawlins to read it aloud.

A stunned silence greeted the reading. Then cheers erupted. His officers flung their hats in the air and slapped one another's backs. Lee had agreed to meet to discuss surrender. If this were arranged, everyone believed the rest of the Confederate forces would also surrender.

Lee arrived before Grant at the McLean house in the village of Appomattox Court House. The village was in southern central Virginia, ninety-two miles west of Richmond and eighteen miles east of Lynchburg, a railroad supply depot. One hundred people lived there; half were slaves.

William McLean was one of the few inhabitants still living in the village, and he had agreed to let the generals use his home as their meeting place. He had lived in Manassas during both battles. After the second battle, he had moved his family to Appomattox to avoid further conflicts.

McLean's three-story brick house was the grandest in the village. It had the biggest parlor in town, with elegant furnishings, befitting the wealthy merchant-trader. Floor to ceiling red velvet drapes, with lace curtains behind, framed the windows. A rag doll sat on the black horsehair couch. The couch looked inviting, but Lee knew that horsehair was bristly and uncomfortable. He seated himself at a small, square marble table near the front window. His military secretary, Lieutenant Colonel Marshall, waited with him.

Lee hoped the meeting would end the fighting and bring the country together again. He had served in the U.S. Army for thirty-six years before the Civil War. His father had been a Revolutionary War hero. His wife was a granddaughter of Martha Washington. Lee loved the United States, but he loved his home state of Virginia more. He would have made any sacrifice to preserve the Union, except for his honor. He believed secession was rebellion, but personal honor had demanded that he return home when Virginia seceded. He could not have fought against his own people.

Lee had never spoken publicly about slavery. Though he thought it was evil and immoral, he shared other Southerners' and many Northerners' feelings that black people were inferior. He believed that the discipline imposed by slave owners on their slaves would ultimately prepare them for better things in their lives.

Two horses nibbled on the grass in the front yard of the house as Grant rode up. Grant recognized Lee's horse, Traveller. He assumed the other horse belonged to one of Lee's officers.

He told his men to wait outside. The caked mud on his boots fell off in clumps as he climbed the seven steps of the wooden porch. His clothing was covered in mud. His beard and hair needed trimming. He had started out from camp a few days ago without his sword or uniform. A soldier's blouse served as his coat. The single-breasted dark blue flannel blouse was unbuttoned in front, and his waistcoat showed underneath. Only his shoulder straps designated his rank. He felt improperly dressed for this important occasion. He hoped Lee would not be offended or think his informality disrespectful. He had thought the meeting too important to wait for his baggage to catch up with him. He consoled himself that at least his headache was gone.

He entered the parlor and was struck with how elegant Lee looked and how immaculately groomed he was. Except for a bit of thinning of his hair, Lee didn't look that much different from when Grant had met him during the Mexican War eighteen years ago.

Mud from Grant's boots left traces on the wine-and-beige patterned carpet as he walked across the room. Grant had been jubilant

upon getting Lee's letter, but he knew how difficult this moment must be for him. Lee was a brilliant general, a mighty foe. He had fought long and valiantly and had suffered much for Virginia. If they could agree on terms of surrender, Grant knew that Lee would hold to his word.

Grant asked the soldier stationed outside the parlor to tell his officers to come in. One by one, he introduced his men to Lee. He saw no emotion on Lee's face until he introduced Ely S. Parker. Lee's eyes lingered on Parker's face. Lee had served in the West with American Indian soldiers, but perhaps he was shocked that one of Grant's officers was an Indian. Parker's Seneca name was Donehogawa; he was the Keeper of the Western Door of the Long House of the Iroquois, the reigning Chief of the Six Nations.

Ever the gentleman, Lee extended his hand. "I am glad to see one real American here."

Parker took Lee's hand and replied, "We are all Americans."

Grant was determined to establish a friendly atmosphere before plunging into the negotiations. "I met you once before while we were serving in Mexico eighteen years ago," he said to Lee. "You came over from General Scott's headquarters to visit Garland's brigade."

Lee's many accomplishments and courage were known to all who had fought in Mexico.

"I think I should have recognized you anywhere," Grant said. He had been twenty-five years old during the Mexican War; Lee was forty then.

Lee knew he had met Grant in Mexico, but he did not remember his face. He politely moved to the subject at hand: "I asked to see you to discuss on what terms you would receive the surrender of my army."

"The terms are those stated in my letter of yesterday," Grant answered. "Your officers and men will be paroled and disqualified from taking up arms again until they are properly exchanged."

Grant saw no sign of emotion on Lee's face. Part of him must be glad that the end had finally come. There had been so much loss on both sides. Family life in the North and South had been shattered. The once splendid cities of Atlanta, Richmond, Petersburg, and Columbia were in ruins. Southern farms, plantations, and forests were burned to the ground. Yes, it was time to end this ugly war that had almost dissolved the Union permanently.

"I hope this may lead to a general suspension of hostilities"— Grant paused—"and be the means of preventing any further loss of life."

Lee nodded in silent agreement. Still, he displayed no emotion. Grant talked on about the prospects for a wider peace. He hoped the other Confederate armies would surrender too.

Lee listened politely and then again brought up the subject of a formal surrender agreement. "Since we have both carefully considered the proper steps to be taken, I would suggest that you commit to writing the terms, so that they may be formally acted upon."

"Very well," Grant said solemnly.

Lieutenant Theodore S. Bowers folded over two thin yellow pages in Lee's leather writing book and inserted carbon sheets between them. Grant put his stylus to the paper. But the words did not come. He wanted to express everything clearly and simply. He wanted no mistaking the terms. Lincoln had told him the peace should have no punishments.

His eyes rested on Lee's handsome sword. What should he do about Confederate officers' horses and weapons? Unlike Union officers, the Confederate officers had brought their own animals and weapons to war. No, he would not humiliate Lee or any of his officers. He would not ask them to surrender their weapons or personal items.

"*In accordance with my letter of the 8th, I propose . . . ,*" Grant wrote. Now the words came easily. It took only a few minutes to write the entire text. Grant read it over, then asked Ely S. Parker to insert a few changes. He gave the agreement to Lee. Lee put on his steel-rimmed spectacles and read silently.

In accordance with my letter of the 8th, I propose to receive the surrender of the Army of Northern Virginia on the following terms: Rolls of all the officers and men to be made in duplicate. One copy will be given to an officer designated by me. The other will be retained by an officer that you designate. The officers will individually give their word not to take up arms against the

*Government of the United States until properly
exchanged.*

*Each company or regimental commander will sign
a similar oath for their men. Arms, artillery, and public
property will be turned over. This will not include the
side-arms of the officers, nor their private horses or baggage. Once this is done, each soldier will be allowed to
return to his home, not to be disturbed so long as they
observe their paroles and the laws in force where they
may reside.*

Very respectfully,
U.S. GRANT, General-in-Chief

"My officers will be happy," said Lee.

"Unless you have some more suggestions, I will have a copy
made," Grant said.

Lee paused. "There is one thing more. Many of my men, not just
the officers, brought their own horses when they joined up. Will
they also be permitted to keep them?"

"The terms as written do not allow this," said Grant. "Only officers are permitted to take their private property." Grant saw Lee's
face tighten. He offered a way out of the dilemma. "Of course, I did
not know how many men in your army brought their animals. I take
it that most of them are small farmers. They will need their horses

to put in crops. I will arrange it this way. I will not change the terms as written, but I will instruct my officers to let anyone who owns animals to take them home."

Lee's facial muscles relaxed. "This will do much toward conciliating our people," he said.

Grant asked Bowers to make copies of the agreement. Bowers started writing but kept making mistakes, so Grant asked Parker to do it. When Parker was finished, Grant read it over and signed it. Parker put the agreement into a large envelope and sealed the envelope with wax. Marshall wrote Lee's acceptance of the terms and gave it to Grant.

Lee turned to the problem of prisoners. He had more than a thousand Union soldiers. He wanted to send them back as soon as possible, for he had no food for them. "I have, indeed, nothing for my own men," he said softly. "They have been living for the last few days on parched corn. And we are badly in need of rations and forage for the animals."

Grant immediately offered food for Lee's men. He expressed regret that he had no feed for the animals.

"I think the rations will be ample," Lee said. "And it will be a great relief, I assure you."

The two generals shook hands. Lee bowed to Grant's officers. It was shortly after three o'clock in the afternoon.

Lee stood on the lowest step of the porch and looked toward the valley where his troops were camped. Grant sensed Lee's sadness in having to return and tell them that he had surrendered.

Robert E. Lee patted Traveller's forelock and mounted. Ulysses S. Grant raised his hat in salute. His officers raised theirs. Lee returned the salute and rode off.

When the news of the surrender reached the Union lines, the soldiers fired off cannons in celebration. Grant ordered the display stopped at once. "The war is over; the rebels are our countrymen again."

The agreement between Lee and Grant on April 9, 1865, effectively ended the war. By mid-May, all remaining Confederate forces had surrendered.

The doll in the room was owned by McLean's seven-year-old daughter, Lucretia. A Union officer took it as a souvenir. Eventually it was returned. You can see it in the museum at the village of Appomattox Court House, which is now a National Historic Park. The park rangers call the doll "the silent witness."

EPILOGUE

On April 14, 1865, the American flag was raised at Fort Sumter. That same day Abraham Lincoln met with his cabinet; Ulysses S. Grant was an invited guest. That night Lincoln and his wife went to Ford's Theatre to see *Our American Cousin.* An angry Southerner, John Wilkes Booth, shot the president. Lincoln died the next day. Andrew Johnson was sworn in as president to face the difficult task of leading the nation in healing its wounds and reconstructing life in the South.

IMPORTANT EVENTS

1787   The United States Constitution, ratified in 1788, allows slavery.

1820   Under the Missouri Compromise, slavery is banned north of 36° 30', except in Missouri, balancing the number of states that permit slavery and those that do not.

1832   South Carolina nullifies the "Tariff of Abominations," which had raised the price of imported goods.

1833   Henry Clay and John C. Calhoun draft a new tariff plan that South Carolina and the other Southern states accept.

1850   The Compromise of 1850 prohibits slave trading in the District of Columbia, accepts California as a free state, and allows western territories to form without deciding on slavery. It includes the Fugitive Slave Act, which makes it illegal for anyone to help a slave escape and states that runaway slaves are to be returned to their owners, even if they are caught in free states.

1852   *Uncle Tom's Cabin*, written by Harriet Beecher Stowe, becomes a best-seller in the North.

1854   The Kansas-Nebraska Act allows people living in territories north of 36° 30' to decide for themselves about the legality of slavery.

1855–1860   Northerners move to the new state of Kansas to keep it free from slavery. Southerners move there to ensure state sovereignty and the right to own slaves. The two sides fight for more than five years.

1857   The Supreme Court's Dred Scott decision declares that slaves are "property," not "persons."

1859   Abolitionist John Brown attacks the U.S. Armory and Arsenal at Harpers Ferry to gain weapons to fight against slavery.

November 6, 1860   Abraham Lincoln is elected the sixteenth president.

December 20, 1860   South Carolina secedes from the Union. Within two months Mississippi, Florida, Alabama, Georgia, Louisiana, and Texas also withdraw.

February 9, 1861   Jefferson Davis is elected president of the Confederate States of America.

April 12–13, 1861   The Civil War begins when the Confederate army takes Fort Sumter.

April 17, 1861   Virginia secedes from the Union.

April 18, 1861   Robert E. Lee rejects the command of the Union armies. Two days later he accepts command of the military and naval forces of Virginia.

May 1861   Arkansas, Tennessee, and North Carolina secede.

July 21, 1861   The South defeats the North in the First Battle of Manassas (First Battle of Bull Run).

August 23, 1861   Eugenia Phillips is arrested as a spy in Washington.

November 18, 1861   Julia Ward Howe writes "The Battle Hymn of the Republic."

March 8–9, 1862   The Battle of USS *Monitor* and CSS *Virginia*, formerly named *Merrimack*, is the first naval battle between ironclad ships. It ends in a draw.

April 25, 1862   Union Admiral David Glasgow Farragut takes New Orleans, Louisiana.

Important Events

May 1, 1862   Union Major General Benjamin F. Butler is appointed commander of New Orleans. President Lincoln removes him on December 23, 1862.

July 3–September 14, 1862   Eugenia Phillips is imprisoned on Ship Island.

August 29–30, 1862   Union forces are defeated at the Second Battle of Manassas (Second Battle of Bull Run).

September 17, 1862   The North wins the Battle of Antietam in Maryland.

January 1, 1863   The Emancipation Proclamation, issued by President Lincoln, frees slaves in Confederate states in rebellion, but does not free slaves in loyal Union states or in those parts of rebel states already occupied by Union forces.

April 2, 1863   Women riot in Richmond, Virginia, over excessively high food prices.

May 4, 1863   Confederate forces win the Battle of Chancellorsville.

May 22–July 4, 1863   General Ulysses S. Grant surrounds Vicksburg, Mississippi, taking the city on Independence Day.

July 3, 1863   The Confederate armies lose the Battle of Gettysburg.

July 18, 1863   The Massachusetts 54th Colored Infantry attacks Fort Wagner, South Carolina.

November 19, 1863   Lincoln delivers the Gettysburg Address.

March 12, 1864   Ulysses S. Grant becomes General-in-Chief of the Union armies.

August 5, 1864   Mobile Bay, Alabama, falls to Admiral David Glasgow Farragut's naval forces.

September 2, 1864   William Tecumseh Sherman captures Atlanta, Georgia.

November 8, 1864   Abraham Lincoln is re-elected president.

January 31, 1865   U.S. Congress approves the Thirteenth Amendment to the Constitution, abolishing slavery. The amendment is submitted to the states remaining in the Union for two-thirds ratification.

February 6, 1865   Robert E. Lee is appointed Commander-in-Chief of the Confederate armies.

March 4, 1865   President Lincoln gives his Second Inaugural Address.

April 2, 1865   Petersburg and Richmond, Virginia, fall to the Union.

April 9, 1865   Lee surrenders at Appomattox Court House, Virginia.

April 12, 1865   Mobile, Alabama, surrenders.

April 14, 1865   John Wilkes Booth assassinates President Abraham Lincoln; Vice President Andrew Johnson is sworn in as president.

May 26, 1865   The last Confederate forces surrender to Major General Edward R. S. Canby, ending the Civil War.

December 6, 1865   The Thirteenth Amendment is ratified by twenty-seven of the thirty-six states. Eight of the remaining states later ratified the amendment; only Mississippi failed to ever ratify it.

THE BATTLE HYMN OF THE REPUBLIC
BY JULIA WARD HOWE

Mine eyes have seen the glory of the coming of the Lord:
He is trampling out the vintage where the grapes of
*　　wrath are stored;*
He hath loosed the fateful lightning of his terrible swift
*　　sword:*
His truth is marching on.

Chorus:

*　　Glory! Glory Hallelujah!*
*　　Glory! Glory Hallelujah!*
*　　Glory! Glory Hallelujah!*
*　　His truth is marching on.*

I have seen Him in the watch-fires of a hundred circling
*　　camps,*
They have builded Him an altar in the evening dews
*　　and damps;*
I can read His righteous sentence by the dim and flar-
*　　ing lamps:*
His day is marching on.
Chorus.

I have read a fiery gospel writ in burnished rows of
*   steel:*
"As ye deal with my condemners, so with you my grace
*   shall deal;*
Let the Hero born of woman crush the serpent with his
*   heel*
Since God is marching on."

Chorus.

He has sounded forth the trumpet that shall never call
*   retreat;*
[He is sifting out the hearts of men before His judgment
*   seat:]*
Oh, be swift my soul, to answer Him! Be jubilant, my
*   feet!*
Our God is marching on.

Chorus.

In the beauty of the lilies Christ was born across the sea,
With a glory in his bosom that transfigures you and me,
As he died to make men holy, let us die to make men
*   free,*
While God is marching on.

Chorus.

SECOND INAUGURAL ADDRESS OF ABRAHAM LINCOLN

Fellow-Countrymen:

At this second appearing to take the oath of the Presidential office there is less occasion for an extended address than there was at the first. Then a statement somewhat in detail of a course to be pursued seemed fitting and proper. Now, at the expiration of four years, during which public declarations have been constantly called forth on every point and phase of the great contest which still absorbs the attention and engrosses the energies of the nation, little that is new could be presented. The progress of our arms, upon which all else chiefly depends, is as well known to the public as to myself, and it is, I trust, reasonably satisfactory and encouraging to all. With high hope for the future, no prediction in regard to it is ventured.

On the occasion corresponding to this four years ago all thoughts were anxiously directed to an impending civil war. All dreaded it, all sought to avert it. While the inaugural address was being delivered from this place, devoted altogether to saving the Union without war, insurgent agents were in the city seeking to destroy it without war—seeking to dissolve the Union and divide effects by negotiation. Both parties deprecated war, but one of them would make war rather than let the nation survive, and the other would accept war rather than let it perish, and the war came.

One-eighth of the whole population were colored slaves, not distributed generally over the Union, but localized in the southern part of it. These slaves constituted a peculiar and powerful interest. All knew that this interest was somehow the cause of the war. To strengthen, perpetuate, and extend this interest was the object for which the insurgents would rend the Union even by war, while the Government claimed no right to do more than to restrict the territorial enlargement of it. Neither party expected for the war the magnitude or the duration which it has already attained. Neither anticipated that the cause of the conflict might cease with or even before the conflict itself should cease. Each looked for an easier triumph, and a result less fundamental and astounding. Both read the same Bible and pray to the same God, and each invokes His aid against the other. It may seem strange that any men should dare to ask a just God's assistance in wringing their bread from the sweat of other men's faces, but let us judge not, that we be not judged. The prayers of both could not be answered. That of neither has been answered fully. The Almighty has His own purposes. "Woe unto the world because of offenses; for it must needs be that offenses come, but woe to that man by whom the offense cometh." If we shall suppose that American slavery is one of those offenses which, in the providence of God, must needs come, but which, having continued through His appointed time, He now wills to remove, and that He gives to both North and South this terrible war as the woe due to those by whom the offense came, shall we discern therein any departure from those divine attributes which the believers in a living God always ascribe to Him? Fondly do we hope, fervently do we pray, that this mighty scourge of war may speedily pass away. Yet, if God wills that it continue until all the wealth piled by the bondsman's two hundred and fifty years of unrequited toil shall be sunk, and until every drop of blood drawn with the lash shall be paid by another drawn with the sword, as was said three thousand years ago, so still it must be said "the judgments of the Lord are true and righteous altogether."

With malice toward none, with charity for all, with firmness in the right as God gives us to see the right, let us strive on to finish the work we are in, to bind up the nation's wounds, to care for him who shall have borne the battle and for his widow and his orphan, to do all which may achieve and cherish a just and lasting peace among ourselves and with all nations.

The inaugural speech above is reproduced from
The Avalon Project at Yale Law School, New Haven, Connecticut.
http://www.yale.edu/lawweb/avalon/presiden/inaug/lincoln2.htm
(included on the Library of Congress site at "official transcription" for
modern text at *http://memory.loc.gov/ammem/pihtml/pi022.html*)
Transcript in Lincoln's hand can be found at the Library of Congress site:
http://memory.loc.gov/cgi-bin/query/r?ammem/pin:@field(NUMBER+pin2202))

ACKNOWLEDGMENTS

As mentioned on page x, the real-life accounts upon which we based these stories were found in diaries, letters, and interviews, and in newspaper articles and books written by historians who spent years researching the past. We compared sources to create the most truthful account of each event. In some stories we were able to track down every detail, and nothing is fictionalized. In other stories we could not document every action or feeling, and some details were re-created based on research as noted. When using original source material, we sometimes changed paragraphing, punctuation, and spelling for readability, or shortened the material without changing its meaning. Refer to the Selected Research Sources, following this section, for more information about the books we used.

Many people helped us find information and/or assured us that the information we had written was accurate. We thank Michael B. Chesson, professor of history, University of Massachusetts, Boston; Dorothy Carter, professor emeritus, Bank Street College of Education; Murella Hebert Powell, local history and genealogy librarian at the Biloxi Public Library, Biloxi, Mississippi; and Margaret Borchers, children's librarian, Monroe Public Library, Monroe, Connecticut, for critiquing the manuscript; Sharon Harrison for her superb research skills and editorial eye; and Kevin Cote for his special reading expertise. We thank our editor, Rosemary Brosnan, for her unflagging commitment to providing children with the fullest possible picture of history.

Acknowledgments

"The Battle Hymn of the Republic" : Julia Ward Howe

Julia Ward Howe witnessed a military review on November 18, 1861, at Bailey's Crossroads in the Seven Corners area of Virginia. In her memoir *Reminiscences 1819–1899*, she did not give specific details of what she saw that day except to say that she traveled to a military review by carriage with the people mentioned in the story, had a picnic brought in a hamper, and left hurriedly during an attack. She did write that the review she witnessed "was discontinued, and we saw a detachment of soldiers gallop to the assistance of a small body of our men in imminent danger of being surrounded and cut off from retreat." She mentioned singing "John Brown's Body" with the retreating Union soldiers and that her minister, James Freeman Clarke, suggested she write "better" words to the song. She also wrote of composing the poem at dawn in her hotel room.

Our research showed that the military reviews of the Grand Army of the Potomac were predictably the same. We re-created this review based on first-person accounts of other reviews, including the one attended by President Lincoln at Bailey's Crossroads on November 20, two days after Julia's visit. Swinton's 1866 *Campaigns of the Army of the Potomac* gives valuable texture about army camp life and topography in the hills of Virginia. Books by Clifford, Grant, Tharp, and Wilson (cited in Selected Research Sources) validate the biographical and story details. (Deborah Pickman Clifford is a descendant of Julia Ward Howe.)

We thank Kimberly M. Akuna, public relations assistant at the Willard InterContinental Washington, for sharing Willard's Sunday, September 29, 1850, "Bill of Fare." *Miss Beecher's Domestic Receipt-Book* by Catharine E.

Beecher provided additional clues about popular luncheon-type foods of the era. Ryan Shephard of the Historical Society of Washington, D.C.'s City Museum led us to the Civil War–era map of Washington, found in Margaret Leech's *Reveille in Washington, 1860–1865*. Additional thanks to Marty Derrig, owner of Black Iron Percherons in Andover, Connecticut, for help with details about horse and carriage travel. Maureen Pihonak, children's librarian at Monroe Public Library, Monroe, Connecticut, and Jenny Shanker, children's librarian at Central Library, Arlington, Virginia, provided other travel details. Jennie Rathbun of Houghton Library at Harvard University helped with early research regarding the contents of the Julia Ward Howe papers housed at the library.

"In Good Spirits": Eugenia Phillips

This story was re-created from the journals and letters of Eugenia Phillips, which detailed these events and her feelings. Local newspapers of the time and the books by Gehman, Massey, Parton, Pember, Ripley, and Sullivan and Powell (cited in Selected Research Sources) provided pertinent details. We' thank experts Jack Judson, curator of the Judson Collection at the Magic Lantern Castle Museum in San Antonio, Texas, and Dick Moore, member of the Magic Lantern Society, for helping us flesh out the magic lantern display mentioned in Eugenia Phillips's memoirs. The slide show that evening is fictionalized, but "Man Eating Rats" was the most popular animated show of the time.

Thanks to Fred Bauman and Cheryl Adams of the Manuscript Division of the Library of Congress and Rachel Canada of the Manuscripts Department at the University of North Carolina at Chapel Hill for their assistance with the

Acknowledgments

Phillips and Meyers Family Papers; to Pamela D. Arceneaux, reference librarian at the Historic New Orleans Collection at the Williams Research Center; to Glen C. Cangelosi, M.D., foundation president, Confederate Memorial Hall's Civil War Museum; to Gail Bishop, chief of interpretation at Gulf Islands National Seashore; and to Murella Hebert Powell, author and local history and genealogy librarian at the Biloxi, Mississippi, Public Library for sharing her considerable knowledge of the life and era of Eugenia Phillips.

"Bread or Blood!": Mary Jackson
The story was created from articles by historians Michael B. Chesson, William J. Kimball, Emory M. Thomas, and Douglas O. Tice, and fleshed out by the doctoral dissertation of Edna Susan Barber. Additional thanks to Frances Pollard of the Virginia Historical Society, Judge Douglas O. Tice of Richmond, who helped validate our pre-story ideas and supplied reprints of newspaper articles of the time, and Mike McKinley, National Park Service, Civil War Battlefield Park, Richmond, Virginia. The speeches of the public officials were taken directly from the newspapers of the time. The women's dialogue at the meeting is fictionalized except in the instance when Mary Jackson told the women not to behave like "a parcel of heathens" and the women called their weapons "persuaders." The cry of "Bread or blood!" is taken directly from Jackson's words to Officer Griffins.

"Flag All Free Without a Slave": William H. Carney
The details and dialogue of this battle are taken from several first-person accounts by soldiers of the Massachusetts 54th, namely, Luis F. Emilio,

117

Corporal James Henry Gooding, and black reporter George E. Stephen, as cited in Selected Research Sources. Letters written by William Carney's comrades Lieutenant Commander William Grace, Company C Private Charles H. Harrison, and Sergeant Major Lewis H. Douglass, son of Frederick Douglass, testified to Carney's merit to receive the Medal of Honor.

While we do not know for certain that William Carney sang the marching song that day, we do know that someone in his regiment wrote the words. Therefore, it is likely that Carney and the other soldiers sang as they waited and marched.

We thank author/historians Virginia Adams and Kathryn Grover for validating our pre-story ideas and Laura Pereira, research assistant at the Old Dartmouth Historical Society Whaling Museum library, and the historians at the New Bedford Historical Society for answering many questions about life in New Bedford prior to the Civil War. Paul Albert Cyr, curator of special collections at the New Bedford Free Public Library, gave invaluable assistance and spoke with one of Carney's descendants.

"Full Speed Ahead!": David Glasgow Farragut
In his biography of his father, Loyall Farragut included his father's letters and descriptions of the battle. Biographies by James P. Duffy and Charles Lee Lewis, as cited in Selected Research Sources, corroborate the details of the attack. Staff at the U.S. Navy Historical Center helped us understand the technology and operation of the ironclads.

Acknowledgments

"With Malice Toward None": Abraham Lincoln and Noah Brooks

The day and activities of Lincoln's second inaugural have been well documented by reporters and by historians. Noah Brooks's newspaper articles, along with articles by other reporters, and the meticulous research in Ronald C. White's book helped us re-create the details and personalities at the inauguration that day. Lincoln's speech has been excerpted; the full speech appears on pages 111–113.

The Surrender: Ulysses S. Grant and Robert E. Lee

The story was created from the memoirs and letters of Robert E. Lee, Ulysses S. Grant, Horace Porter, and Ely S. Parker. William H. Armstrong's biography of Ely S. Parker expanded on important details. Historians Bruce Catton, J. F. C. Fuller, and Brooks D. Simpson fleshed out military strategy and the personalities of the two generals. Emory M. Thomas's biography of Robert E. Lee was particularly helpful. Special thanks to Jeffrey M. Flannery, manuscript reference specialist, Manuscript Division at the Library of Congress, for digging up Ely Parker's first-person narrative. A visit to the National Park Service Historic Site of Appomattox Court House enabled us to meet historian Patrick Schroeder and curator Joe Williams, who answered numerous questions.

SELECTED RESEARCH SOURCES

Adams, Virginia Matzke. *On the Altar of Freedom, A Black Soldier's Civil War Letters from the Front (Corporal James Henry Gooding)*. Amherst: The University of Massachusetts Press, 1991.

Appomattox Court House, National Historical Park, Virginia, produced by the Division of Publications, Harpers Ferry Center, National Park Service, U.S. Department of the Interior, Washington, D.C.

Armstrong, William H. *Warrior in Two Camps: Ely S. Parker, Union General and Seneca Chief.* Syracuse, NY: Syracuse University Press, 1978.

Ashkenazi, Elliott, ed. *The Civil War Diary of Clara Solomon, Growing Up in New Orleans, 1861–1862*. Baton Rouge: Louisiana State University Press, 1995.

Barber, Edna Susan. *"Sisters of the Capital": White Women in Richmond, Virginia, 1860–1880*. Doctoral dissertation, University of Maryland at College Park, 1997.

Bearss, Edwin C. *The Historic Resource Study, Ship Island, Harrison County, Mississippi*. U.S. Department of the Interior, National Park Service, Denver Service Center, 1984.

Beecher, Catharine E. *Miss Beecher's Domestic Receipt-Book*. Mineola, NY: Dover Publications, 2001.

Beller, Susan Provost. *Confederate Ladies of Richmond*. Brookfield, CT: Twenty-First Century Books, 1999.

Blanton, DeAnne, and Lauren M. Cook. *They Fought Like Demons: Women Soldiers in the American Civil War*. Baton Rouge: Louisiana State University Press, 2002.

Bragg, Rick. "In New Orleans, Sweetness Is All a Matter of Civic Pride." *New York Times*. July 15, 2002.

Burlingame, Michael, ed. *Lincoln Observed: Civil War Dispatches of Noah Brooks*. Baltimore, MD: The Johns Hopkins University Press, 1998.

Catton, Bruce. *The Civil War*. Boston: Houghton Mifflin, 1988.

———. *U.S. Grant and the American Military Tradition*. Boston: Little, Brown, 1954.

Chesson, Michael B. "Harlots or Heroines? A New Look at the Richmond Bread Riot." *The Virginia Magazine of History and Biography*, April 1984.

Clifford, Deborah Pickman. *Mine Eyes Have Seen the Glory: A Biography of Julia Ward Howe*. Boston: Little, Brown, 1978.

Dabney, Virginius. *Richmond: The Story of a City*. Charlottesville: University of Virginia Press, 1991.

Donald, David Herbert. *Lincoln*. New York: Simon & Schuster, 1996.

Duffy, James P. *Lincoln's Admiral*. New York: John Wiley & Sons, 1997.

Emilio, Luis F. *A Brave Black Regiment: History of the Fifty-Fourth Regiment of Massachusetts Volunteer Infantry, 1863–1865*. New York: Arno Press and *The New York Times*, 1969.

Farragut, Loyall. *Life of David Glasgow Farragut*. New York: D. Appleton, 1879.

Fuller, J. F. C. *Grant & Lee: A Study in Personality and Generalship*. Bloomington: Indiana University Press, 1957.

Gehman, Mary. *Women and New Orleans*. New Orleans, LA: Margaret Media, 1988.

Grant, Mary H. *Private Woman, Public Person, An Account of the Life of Julia*

Ward Howe from 1819 to 1868. Brooklyn, NY: Carlson Publishing, 1994.

Grant, Ulysses S. *Memoirs and Selected Letters: Personal Memoirs of U.S. Grant, Selected Letters 1839–1865*. New York: Library of America, 1990.

Hearn, Chester G. *Admiral David Glasgow Farragut: The Civil War Years*. Annapolis, MD: Naval Institute Press, 1998.

Holzer, Harold. *Lincoln Seen and Heard*. Lawrence: University Press of Kansas, 2000.

Howe, Julia Ward. *Reminiscences, 1819–1899*. Boston: Houghton, Mifflin, 1899.

Kimball, Gregg D. *American City, South Place: A Cultural History of Antebellum Richmond*. Athens: The University of Georgia Press, 2000.

Leonard, Elizabeth D. *All the Daring of the Soldier: Women of the Civil War Armies*. New York: W. W. Norton, 1999.

Lewis, Charles Lee. *David Glasgow Farragut: Our First Admiral*. Annapolis, MD: U.S. Naval Institute, 1943.

Massey, Mary Elizabeth. *Bonnet Brigades*. New York: Alfred A. Knopf, 1966.

McPherson, James M. *Battle Cry of Freedom*. New York: Ballantine Books, 1989.

———. *Marching Toward Freedom, Blacks in the Civil War, 1861–1865*. New York: Facts on File, 1991.

Melia, Tamara Moser. *"Damn the Torpedoes": A Short History of U.S. Naval Mine Countermeasures, 1777–1991*. Washington, DC: Naval Historical Center, 1991.

Oates, Stephen B. *Abraham Lincoln, the Man Behind the Myths*. New York: Harper & Row, 1984.

Paludan, Phillip S. *The Presidency of Abraham Lincoln*. Lawrence: University Press of Kansas, 1994.

Parton, James. *General Butler in New Orleans, History of the Administration of the Department of the Gulf in the Year 1862*. Boston: Fields, Osgood, 1871.

Pember, Phoebe Yates. *A Southern Woman's Story*. Jackson, TN: McCowat-Mercer Press, 1959.

Phillips, Philip. *Journal of Mrs. Eugenia Phillips, 1861–1862*. Philip Phillips Family Papers, Library of Congress, Manuscript Division.

Proctor, Samuel, ed., with Louis Schmier and Malcolm Stern. *Jews of the South: Selected Essays from the Southern Jewish Historical Society*. Macon, GA.: Mercer University Press, 1984.

Ripley, Eliza. *Social Life in Old New Orleans*. Gretna, LA: Pelican Publishing, 1998.

Simpson, Brooks D. *Let Us Have Peace: Ulysses S. Grant and the Politics of War and Reconstruction, 1861–1868*. Chapel Hill: University of North Carolina Press, 1991.

Staudenraus, P. J. *Mr. Lincoln's Washington: Selections from the Writings of Noah Brooks, Civil War Correspondent*. London: Thomas Yoseloff, 1967.

Stephens, George E. *A Voice of Thunder: The Civil War Letters of George E. Stephens*, edited by Donald Yacovone. Urbana: University of Illinois Press, 1997.

Sullivan, Charles L., and Murella Hebert Powell. *The Mississippi Gulf Coast, Portrait of a People*. Sun Valley, CA: American Historical Press, 1999.

Swinton, William. *Campaigns of the Army of the Potomac*. New York: Charles B. Richardson, 1866.

Tharp, Louise Hall. *Three Saints and a Sinner: Julia Ward Howe, Louisa, Annie and Sam Howe*. Boston: Little, Brown, 1956.

Thomas, Emory M. "The Richmond Bread Riot of 1863." *Virginia Cavalcade*, Summer 1968.

———. *Robert E. Lee: A Biography*. New York: W. W. Norton, 1995.

Tice, Douglas O. "'Bread or Blood!' The Richmond Bread Riot." *Civil War Times Illustrated*, February 1974.

West, Jr., Richard S. *Lincoln's Scapegoat General: A Life of Benjamin F. Butler, 1818–1893*. Boston: Houghton Mifflin, 1965.

White, Jr., Ronald C. *Lincoln's Greatest Speech: The Second Inaugural*. New York: Simon & Schuster, 2002.

Wilson, Edmund. *Patriotic Gore: Studies in the Literature of the American Civil War*. New York: Oxford University Press, 1962.

BOOKS AND WEBSITES FOR
YOUNG READERS

Nonfiction

Adelson, Bruce. *David Farragut: Union Admiral*. New York: Chelsea House, 2001.

Chang, Ina. *A Separate Battle: Women and the Civil War*. New York: Puffin Books, 1991.

Collier, James Lincoln. *With Every Drop of Blood*. New York: Bantam Doubleday Dell, 1996.

Colman, Penny. *Spies!: Women in the Civil War*. Newton, OH: F & W Publications, 1992.

Dolan, Jr., Edward F. *American Civil War: A House Divided*. Brookfield, CT: Millbrook, 1997.

Egger-Bovet, Howard, James J. Rawls, and Marlene Smith-Baranzini. *Book of the American Civil War*. New York: Little Brown, 1998.

Freedman, Russell. *Lincoln: A Photobiography*. Boston: Houghton Mifflin, 1989.

Fritz, Jean. *Just a Few Words, Mr. Lincoln: The Story of the Gettysburg Address*. New York: Grosset & Dunlap Putnam, 1993.

Hakim, Joy. *War, Terrible War* (A History of US Series #6). London: Oxford University Press, 1998.

Haskins, Jim. *Black, Blue & Gray: African Americans in the Civil War*. New York: Simon & Schuster, 1998.

Herbert, Janis. *The Civil War for Kids: A History with 21 Activities*. Chicago: Chicago Review Press, 1999.

Holzer, Harold, ed. *Abraham Lincoln the Writer: A Treasury of His Greatest Speeches and Letters*. Honesdale, PA: Boyds Mill Press, 2000.

McGovern, Ann. *If You Grew Up with Abraham Lincoln*. New York: Scholastic, 1992.

McKissack, Patricia C. and Frederick L. *Black Hands, White Sails: The Story of African-American Whalers*. New York: Scholastic, 1999.

Murphy, Jim. *The Boys' War: Confederate and Union Soldiers Talk About the Civil War*. New York: Clarion Books, 1990.

Rappaport, Doreen. *Escape from Slavery: Five Journeys to Freedom*. New York: HarperCollins, 1988.

———. *No More! Stories and Songs of Slave Resistance*. Cambridge, MA: Candlewick Press, 2003.

Reit, Seymour V. *Behind Rebel Lines: The Incredible Story of Emma Edmonds, Civil War Spy*. New York: Harcourt, 2001.

Sandler, Martin W. *Civil War, A Library of Congress Book*. New York: HarperCollins, 1996.

Savage, Douglas J. *Women in the Civil War*. New York: Chelsea House, 2000.

Shorto, Russell. *David Farragut and the Great Naval Blockade*. Englewood Cliffs, NJ: Silver Burdett Press, 1991.

Wisler, G. Clifton. *When Johnny Went Marching: Young Americans Fight the Civil War*. New York: HarperCollins, 2001.

Fiction

Bartoletti, Susan. *No Man's Land, A Young Soldier's Story.* New York: Scholastic, 1999.

Crist-Evans, Craig. *Moon over Tennessee, A Boy's Civil War Diary.* Boston: Houghton Mifflin, 1999.

Osborne, Mary Pope. *After the Rain, Virginia's Civil War Diary: Book Two.* New York: Scholastic, 2001.

————. *Civil War on Sunday.* New York: Random House, 2000.

————. *My Brother's Keeper, Virginia's Diary.* New York: Scholastic, 2000.

Paulsen, Gary. *Soldier's Heart, Being the Story of the Enlistment and Due Service of the Boy Charley Goddard in the First Minnesota Volunteers.* New York: Dell Laurel-Leaf, 1998.

Websites

Civil War Defenses of Washington
www.nps.gov/cwdw/

Fort Sumter National Monument
http://www. nps.gov/fosu

Long Bridge (as traveled by Julia Ward Howe)
www.gmu.edu/library/specialcollections/longbridge.gif

Magic-Lantern Theater: History of the Magic Lantern
www.magiclanternshows.com/history.htm

The McLean House/Appomattox Court House NHM
www.nps.gov/apco/mchs.htm

Memorial Hall Confederate Museum
www.confederatemuseum.com

Mobile Bay
www.history.navy.mil/photos/sh-us-cs/csa-sh/csash-sz/tenn-k.htm

Time Line of the Civil War
www.memory.loc.gov/ammem/cwphtml/tl1861.html

Willard's Hotel
www.mrlincolnswhitehouse.org/inside.asp?ID=184&subjectID=4

INDEX